The Observer's Pocket Series

AUTOMOBILES

About the Book

The success of this title as an outstanding reference book providing illustrations and data of the world's most significant production cars has been maintained for almost a quarter of a century. In the 24th edition maximum coverage has been devoted to those models which have been presented for the first time or substantially changed for 1980–1981.

The book has been compiled with both the enthusiast and the professional in mind and has been designed to meet the needs of anyone requiring a handy book containing concise information and clear illustrations for quick identification and reference.

About the Author

John Blunsden is one of Britain's foremost motoring writers with a career as an author, journalist, broadcaster, editor and publisher spanning 25 years and embracing all aspects of the motoring scene. A past Chairman of The Guild of Motoring Writers and a founder member of the International Racing Press Association, he now devotes much of his time to the world of motoring books as Managing Director of Motor Racing Publications Ltd (publishers) and Connoisseur Carbooks (specialist book-sellers) and as consultant to other publishing houses in the motoring book field.

The Observer's Book of
AUTOMOBILES

Compiled by
JOHN BLUNSDEN

FREDERICK WARNE
LONDON

NOTE

*The specifications contained in this book were collated
on the basis of material available to the compiler up to the
end of October 1980. All information is subject to change
and/or cancellation during the course of the model year.
Although every effort has been made to ensure correct-
ness in compiling this book responsibility for inaccuracies
and omissions cannot be accepted by the compilers and
publishers.*

LIBRARY OF CONGRESS CATALOG
CARD NO. 62–9807

ISBN 0 7232 1617 7

Typeset by CCC, printed and bound in
Great Britain by William Clowes (Beccles) Limited,
Beccles and London

INTRODUCTION

The changes in information and presentation made to the previous edition of *The Observer's Book of Automobiles*, which were aimed at making this very popular pocket book even more interesting and valuable as a guide to the cars on our roads, have been maintained for this current edition following the favourable response from many of our regular readers.

Inevitably it is impossible to cover the entire spectrum of world production of cars within the compass of less than 200 pages, and it has been necessary to be selective in the choice of entries. In doing so, prime importance has been given to those cars which have been introduced during the past year or so, as well as those which have undergone significant changes in specification during that period. At the same time, those models which have continued virtually unchanged have not been overlooked where they represent an important segment of the total market.

In these days most manufacturers design and produce cars for export sales as much as for their home market, and often specifications have to be changed to meet local demands and regulations. As far as possible, where a car is available on the British market it is the UK specification which has been quoted, even though this may be at variance with the specification in the country of manufacture. Not all of the models described and illustrated, however, are available in the UK, but such cars as have been included despite this have earned an entry because of their significance to the world automotive scene as a whole.

The period between the 'signing off' of a new car for production and its appearance in the showrooms is considerably longer than that between the passing of a book for press and its appearance on the bookshelves. Consequently, a number of models which might otherwise have been featured in this edition have had to be omitted either because they have yet to be revealed to the public, or because the relevant data on them was not available at the time this book went to press. Similarly, other cars which ordinarily would have warranted an entry have been excluded because of a pending change of specification which would have made the entry obsolete.

As competition between rival manufacturers intensifies there is a growing trend towards the marketing of 'limited edition'

5

versions of their regular product lines, which often offer better value for money and a higher-than-usual specification. For the most part these variants have been ignored, unless there has been a strong chance of their conversion into a long-term selling line.

In preparing the data which is published on the following pages considerable help has been provided by the manufacturers and/or their importers or concessionaires concerned, for which the author and publishers are most grateful. It is only whilst researching data of this type, however, that one discovers the degree to which inconsistencies have crept into factual material which has been assembled over the years.

For example, not every manufacturer uses precisely the same method of horsepower calculation, and confusion is compounded in conversion from metric to imperial measures, or vice versa, in so far as there are subtle differences in the DIN and ISO 1585 International Standards used for these calculations and conversions. In all cases it will be found that the output and torque figures quoted (in both metric and imperial units) in this book are either those obtained from factory sources or calculations which approximate very closely indeed to them.

Another area of considerable discrepancy concerns overall dimensions and unladen weight, the former, perhaps, because small changes in things like bumpers and side rubbing strips are seemingly ignored in certain quarters, and the latter because once again there is an inconsistency in the method of measurement. The figures quoted have been taken as the most accurate available, and should be found to be within acceptable tolerances.

One final word of advice. The specification of seemingly unchanging cars is usually undergoing subtle improvement all the time, and manufacturers will never lose the opportunity to uprate their cars whenever they can afford to do so. Conversely, in an effort to contain prices in an inflationary economic climate, car producers will occasionally 'detune' the specification of certain of their models. It is advisable, therefore, when using this book as a guide to car purchase, as distinct from a means of expanding one's interest in cars generally, to augment it with the latest sales literature obtainable from the relevant dealer. Meanwhile, events in the car-manufacture world will be monitored very closely during the coming year, for even as this book comes off the printing presses some of the content of the next edition of *The Observer's Book of Automobiles* is already being assembled.

The year in retrospect

If 1979 was the year during which the world's motor industry became united on a path towards energy conservation through the production of smaller and more fuel-efficient cars, 1980 can be marked down as the year during which this trend was developed against a background of the worst recession to hit the industry since the early 1930s.

It was the year during which even the traditionally strongest manufacturers, the multi-nationals such as General Motors and Ford, found themselves in a crisis of over-capacity and when even the most drastic surgery failed to stop the declaration of the worst financial figures for many years. Factory closures and short-time working became the norm, both in North America and in Europe, as the industry tried to readjust output to a markedly reduced demand and a market which became so cost-conscious that in many instances substantial and costly inducements were necessary to maintain showroom traffic at even a tolerable level.

Against this sombre background, however, the industry put on a brave face at the various international exhibitions, and public interest was continually being stimulated by the introduction of interesting new models or more attractive variants of existing designs. These, almost invariably, provided further evidence of the industry's continuing success to develop more efficient designs, and if nothing else the world recession, stifling though its effect may have been on the overall car market, did at least force the industry to take a very careful look at its product line, weed out the dead wood and consequently present a significantly more appealing catalogue.

For the British industry and market the year was a more than usually interesting one in new product terms, the highlight of the year, if only for its significance to the future of British Leyland, being the arrival of the long-awaited and much talked about Mini Metro. This car has entered the most competitive of all sectors of the market, and one where inevitably the profit per unit cannot be high. It is not the salvation of this very diversified car manufacturing complex, therefore, but rather the means for beginning the recovery process, which hopefully will be continued at an accelerating pace through the introduction of other new models, notably the Japanese-designed car codenamed at BL as the Bounty, and the eventual Marina/Ital replacement, coded the

LC10. Meanwhile, the Metro has been favourably received as an imaginative design which, if backed with quality and reliability, should make it a formidable contender in its class. It is interesting that amongst the variants is one which combines a high level of specification with a small high-compression engine linked to high gearing to provide extreme economy.

Preceding the Metro by only a few days, the new Ford Escort follows the pioneering work of the Fiesta in taking Ford into the mainstream of the front-wheel-drive market where it can compete with European rivals like the VW Golf, Opel Kadett, Fiat Ritmo/Strada and Renault 14 as well as the Japanese newcomers such as the remarkably similar Mazda 323 range. As before, the Escort is not just a new car but a whole range of new cars, from economy model to high-performance derivative and with a wide selection of trim levels.

Another significant development in 1980 was the emergence of a new Rolls-Royce, significant insofar as it is virtually the same size as the Silver Shadow which it replaces, and with the same power unit. Nevertheless, the new bodywork, apart from giving the car a much more up-to-date appearance with more rounded lines, is also aerodynamically superior, and as a result the new car is an important step more economical than its predecessor. The Rolls-Royce philosophy, in this respect, has been similar to that of Mercedes-Benz in creating their latest S-series cars, which first appeared towards the end of 1979, and which are again of similar size to the cars which they replace. In this case, however, new and smaller engines are called upon to provide similar levels of performance to discontinued larger power units. One interesting detail of the Rolls-Royce announcement was the introduction of the Mulsanne name for the Bentley variant, surely the first step in a long programme aimed eventually at re-establishing the sporting image of this famous name.

Some worthwhile improvements in engine design do not make large headlines, and so the latest version of the glorious Jaguar V12 5.3-litre engine, more powerful as well as more economical than the previous example, came on stream almost unnoticed, but must be rated an important step in technological development nonetheless. The search for more fuel efficiency does not always mean smaller engines or modification of those which remain the same size. Lotus are an example of a company who have found that the best way is to increase displacement, in this case from 2-litres to 2.2-litres, while Opel have decided to replace their 2.8-

litre Senator with a 3-litre version equipped with a single carburettor (to supplement the top-of-the-range fuel-injected car).

As further evidence that the larger car (in European terminology) is far from dead, Talbot's major announcement towards the end of 1980 was of a forthcoming replacement for the old Chrysler 2-litre in the form of a more spacious model, the Tagora, which is to be offered during 1981 with a range of power units up to 2.7-litres—an interesting introduction, this, in that it would seem to put Talbot in a sector of the market already occupied by the Peugeot 604, from another arm of the PSA combine. Perhaps inter-divisional rivalry between these two companies is to be encouraged despite the closing of the marketing ties between them.

If there was one predominant technical trend during 1980 it was the rash of new cars with turbocharged engines. The remarkable four-wheel-drive Audi Quattro arrived early in the year as a car clearly destined for international rallying, while it was closely followed by Renault's 5 Turbo, a fascinating yet different approach to the same task. These two cars will doubtless make many headlines in the sporting sphere in the months and perhaps years ahead, but will remain relatively small fry in production terms. Of more significance, therefore, was the introduction of the Renault 18 Turbo, a car which brings this form of propulsion right into the mainstream of the passenger car market, and it will be interesting to monitor the level of acceptance it achieves amongst buyers attracted by this method of providing high performance when it is needed, together with the inherent economy of a small-displacement engine.

The Audi Quattro's body shape has since appeared in a more conventional guise to clothe a front-wheel-drive coupe of high specification, while Renault once again demonstrated their current concern for good aerodynamics with the introduction of a new range of coupes called the Fuego, clearly aimed at the market originally identified by Ford with their Capris.

Inevitably, the small specialist manufacturers found 1980 in the main to be a worrying year, not so much due to any lack of appeal of their products, but rather because of the financial difficulties of relating profitability to small output at a time of high inflation and, in the case of the UK, an over-valued currency. A bright spot in this field, however, was provided by TVR, who not only announced, in their Tasmin two-seater coupe, far and away the most attractive car they had made to date, but who followed it through with two-plus-two and convertible derivatives before the year was out. With BL doing far better with the open version of the TR7 than they ever achieved with the coupe, the demand for genuine open-air motoring no longer seems to be seriously in question, at least in the warmer climates such as are to be found on the American West Coast and in southern Europe.

During 1980 the popularity of diesel-engined passenger cars seemed to increase in some markets yet remain relatively stagnant in others. In the United States compression-ignition engines have become relatively commonplace, and it may surprise European motorists to know that the majority of cars in the new Mercedes-Benz S-class destined for the USA during the next year will be diesel-powered. However, this form of propulsion has not always been matched by a ready availability of fuel, and in some parts of the United States it is necessary to plan long journeys in diesel-powered cars with a certain amount of care.

Towards the end of 1980 there were the first signs of a subtle improvement in the market for the depressed United States auto industry, undoubtedly as a response to the gradual integration of European and Japanese-designed models into the domestic manufacturers' catalogue. In Europe, too, there were one or two signs of a slight improvement in the market to relieve the gloom of previous months, but on the Continent of Europe there was increasing concern by local manufacturers at the inroads made into their home markets by imported Japanese cars—a problem all too familiar in Britain for some years. With a markedly improved level of sophistication, the Japanese product was now able to meet its European rivals face-to-face and be judged a worthy competitor in technological as well as marketing terms, and as the European motor industry moved into 1981 there was the real prospect that some form of protection would be necessary, preferably on a voluntary level such as had been pioneered by Japan and the United Kingdom. During the year ahead, in fact, the foundations for the industry's future may well be influenced as much by what takes place around the negotiating table as that which appears on the drawing board and the test laboratory. Without doubt, 1981 will be a year for crucial decisions.

INTERNATIONAL REGISTRATION LETTERS

These consist of one, two or three letters of the same size, usually in black, set on a white oval background. They indicate the country of origin as set out below, and are displayed by cars which are being driven in foreign countries.

They have also been used throughout this book to indicate countries of manufacture.

Not all countries subscribe to this system of identification, however. For example, a plate bearing the letters TT (*Titre Temporaire*) shows that the owner has temporarily registered in France, though he may have come from another country originally. The letters following TT indicate the particular district of France where the registration was taken out.

Those plates with prefixes from QA to QS are issued by the R.A.C. or the A.A. in this country to vehicles temporarily imported from abroad. Numbers prefaced by EE indicate a first temporary registration for touring from Italy.

Cars used by High Commissioners in this country carry small plates bearing the letters HC, and those used by Foreign Embassies and Legations have a plate with the letters CD in addition to their registration plates.

The letters given in brackets are proposed new signs which are being or will be introduced. An asterisk denotes a country in which the rule of the road is drive on the left; otherwise drive on the right.

A (AT)	Austria	CO	Colombia
ADN (YD)	Democratic Yemen (formerly Aden)*	CR	Costa Rica
		CS	Czechoslovakia
AFG (AF)	Afghanistan	CY	Cyprus*
AL	Albania	D (DE)	German Federal Republic
AND (AD)	Andorra		
AUS (AU)	Australia*	DDR (DD)	German Democratic Republic
B (BE)	Belgium		
BDS (BB)	Barbados*	DK	Denmark
BG	Bulgaria	DOM (DO)	Dominican Republic
BH (BZ)	Belize (formerly British Honduras)	DY	Benin (formerly Dahomey)
BR	Brazil	DZ	Algeria
BRN (BH)	Bahrain	E (ES)	Spain (including African territories)
BRU (BN)	Brunei*		
BS	Bahamas*	EAK (KE)	Kenya*
BUR (BU)	Burma	EAT (TZ)	Tanzania (formerly Tanganyika)
C (CU)	Cuba		
CDN (CA)	Canada	EAU (UG)	Uganda*
CH	Switzerland	EAZ (TZ)	Tanzania (formerly Zanzibar)*
CI	Ivory Coast		
CL (LK)	Sri Lanka (formerly Ceylon)*	EC	Ecuador

Code	Country
ET (EG)	Arab Republic of Egypt
F (FR)	France (including overseas departments and territories)
FJI (FJ)	Fiji•
FL (LI)	Liechtenstein
GB	United Kingdom of Great Britain and Northern Ireland•
GBA	Alderney• ⎫
GBG	Guernsey• ⎬ Channel
GBJ	Jersey• ⎭ Islands
GBM	Isle of Man
GBZ (GI)	Gibraltar
GCA (GT)	Guatemala
GH	Ghana
GR	Greece
GUY (GY)	Guyana• (formerly British Guiana)
H (HU)	Hungary
HK	Hong Kong•
HKJ (JO)	Jordan
I (IT)	Italy
IL	Israel
IND (IN)	India•
IR	Iran
IRL (IE)	Ireland•
IRQ (IQ)	Iraq
IS	Iceland
J (JP)	Japan•
JA (JM)	Jamaica•
K (KH)	Kampuchea (Cambodia)
KWT (KW)	Kuwait
L (LU)	Luxembourg
LAO (LA)	Laos
LAR (LY)	Libya
LB (LR)	Liberia
LS	Lesotho (formerly Basutoland)•
M (MT)	Malta•
MA	Morocco
MAL (MY)	Malaysia•
MC	Monaco
MEX (MX)	Mexico
MS (MU)	Mauritius•
MW	Malawi•
N (NO)	Norway
NA (AN)	Netherlands Antilles
NIC (NI)	Nicaragua
NL	Netherlands
NZ	New Zealand•
P (PT)	Portugal
P (AO)	Angola
P (CV)	Cape Verde Islands
P (MZ)	Mozambique•
P (GN)	Guinea-Bissau
P (TP)	Timor
P (ST)	São Tomé and Principe
PA	Panama
PAK (PK)	Pakistan•
PE	Peru
PL	Poland
PY	Paraguay
R (RO)	Romania
RA (AR)	Argentina
RB (BW)	Botswana (formerly Bechuanaland)•
RC (TW)	Taiwan (Republic of China)
RCA (CF)	Central African Republic
RCB (CG)	Congo
RCH (CL)	Chile
RH (HT)	Haiti
RI (ID)	Indonesia•
RIM (MR)	Mauritania
RL (LB)	Lebanon
RM (MG)	Madagascar
RMM (ML)	Mali
ROK (KP)	Korea (Republic of)
RP (PH)	Philippines
RSM (SM)	San Marino
RSR (RH)	Rhodesia (formerly Southern Rhodesia)•
RU (BI)	Burundi
RWA (RW)	Rwanda
S (SE)	Sweden
SD (SZ)	Swaziland•
SF (FI)	Finland
SGP (SG)	Singapore•
SME (SR)	Surinam (formerly Dutch Guiana)•
SN	Senegal
SU	Union of Soviet Socialist Republics
SWA	South West Africa•
SY (SC)	Seychelles•
SYR (SY)	Syria
T (TH)	Thailand•
TG	Togo
TN	Tunisia
TR	Turkey
TT	Trinidad and Tobago•
U (UY)	Uruguay
USA (US)	United States of America
V (VA)	Vatican City
VN (VD)	Vietnam (Republic of)

WAG (GM)	Gambia	WV (VC)	St Vincent
WAL (SL)	Sierra Leone		(Windward Islands)*
WAN (NG)	Nigeria	YU	Yugoslavia
WD (DM)	Dominica*⎫ Wind-	YV (VE)	Venezuela
WG (GD)	Granada* ⎬ ward	Z	Zambia*
WL (LC)	St Lucia* ⎭ Islands	ZA	South Africa*
WS	Western Samoa*	ZR (ZM)	Zaire (formerly Congo Kinshasha)

ALFA ROMEO (I)

Alfasud 1.5

Identification: Extensively revised version of Alfasud four-door saloon with redesigned interior, different front, rear and side exterior trim and additional rustproofing.

Engine: Front-mounted four-cylinder horizontally opposed with belt-driven overhead camshafts and Weber carburettor. Bore × stroke 84 × 67.2 mm, displacement 1490 cc. Output 63 kW (84 bhp) @ 5800 rpm, torque 123 Nm (89 lb ft) @ 3500 rpm.

Transmission: Single-dry-plate clutch and five-speed manual gearbox. Front-wheel drive.

Suspension: Front, independent with MacPherson struts, coil springs, telescopic shock absorbers and anti-roll bar. Rear, dead axle with Watt linkage, Panhard rod, coil springs and telescopic shock absorbers.

Steering: Rack and pinion.

Brakes: Discs front and rear, servo-assisted.

Tyres: 165/70 SR–13.

Dimensions: Length 3934 mm (154.9 in), width 1590 mm (62.6 in), height 1369 mm (53.9 in), wheelbase 2456 mm (96.7 in).

Unladen weight: 880 kg (1940 lb).

Notes: Standard equipment includes front spoiler, rear central armrest with luggage compartment access hole and door-protection mouldings.

ALFA ROMEO (I)

Alfasud Ti 1.5

Identification: Revised model at upper end of Alfasud range with modified styling incorporating front and rear spoilers and powered by Sprint Veloce engine.

Engine: Front-mounted four-cylinder horizontally opposed with belt-driven overhead camshafts and two twin-choke Weber carburettors. Bore × stroke 84 × 67.2 mm, displacement 1490 cc. Output 71 kW (95 bhp) @ 5800 rpm, torque 133 Nm (96 lb ft) @ 4000 rpm.

Transmission: Single-dry-plate clutch and five-speed manual gearbox. Front-wheel drive.

Suspension: Front, independent with MacPherson struts, coil springs, telescopic shock absorbers and anti-roll bar. Rear, dead axle with Watt linkage, Panhard rod, coil springs and telescopic shock absorbers.

Steering: Rack and pinion.

Brakes: Discs front and rear, servo-assisted.

Tyres: 165/70 SR–13.

Dimensions: Length 3934 mm (154.9 in), width 1623 mm (63.9 in), height 1369 mm (53.9 in), wheelbase 2456 mm (96.7 in).

Unladen weight: 880 kg (1940 lb).

Notes: Standard equipment includes central rear armrest and luggage compartment access plate for stowage of long items.

ALFA ROMEO (I)   Giulietta 2.0

Identification: Addition to Giulietta range, supplementing 1.6-litre and 1.8-litre models and powered by 2-litre Alfetta engine.

Engine: Front-mounted four-cylinder in-line with twin chain-driven overhead camshafts and twin Dellorto or Solex carburettors. Bore × stroke 84 × 88.5 mm, displacement 1962 cc. Output 97 kW (130 bhp) @ 5400 rpm, torque 181 Nm (130 lb ft) @ 4000 rpm.

Transmission: Single-dry-plate clutch and five-speed manual gearbox, rear-mounted. Rear-wheel drive.

Suspension: Front, independent with wishbones, torsion bars, telescopic shock absorbers and anti-roll bar. Rear, de Dion tube with trailing arms, Watt linkage, coil springs, telescopic shock absorbers and anti-roll bar.

Steering: Rack and pinion.

Brakes: Discs front and rear, servo-assisted.

Tyres: 185/65 HR–14.

Dimensions: Length 4210 mm (165.8 in), width 1650 mm (65 in), height 1400 mm (55.1 in), wheelbase 2510 mm (98.8 in).

Unladen weight: 1100 kg (2424 lb).

Notes: Standard equipment includes reclining seats and alloy wheels. Air-conditioning optional extra.

ALFA ROMEO (I) Alfetta GTV/SE

Identification: High-specification UK-market version of GTV coupe derived from Alfetta four-door saloon and featuring rear-mounted gearbox.

Engine: Front-mounted four-cylinder in-line with twin chain-driven overhead camshafts and twin Dellorto or Solex carburettors. Bore × stroke 84 × 88.5 mm, displacement 1962 cc. Output 97 kW (130 bhp) @ 5300 rpm, torque 180 Nm (130 lb ft) @ 4000 rpm.

Transmission: Single-dry-plate clutch and five-speed manual gearbox. Rear-wheel drive.

Suspension: Front, independent with wishbones, torsion bars, telescopic shock absorbers and anti-roll bar. Rear, de Dion axle with trailing arms, Watt linkage, coil springs, telescopic shock absorbers and anti-roll bar.

Steering: Rack and pinion.

Brakes: Discs front and rear, servo-assisted.

Tyres: 185/70 HR–14.

Dimensions: Length 4153 mm (163.5 in), width 1664 mm (65.5 in), height 1334 mm (52.5 in), wheelbase 2413 mm (95 in).

Unladen weight: 1080 kg (2380 lb).

Notes: Standard equipment includes alloy wheels, tinted glass, electric window lifts, rear screen wash/wipe, stereo radio/cassette player, front and rear fog lamps, sun roof and velvet-trimmed seats.

ALFA ROMEO (I)

Alfa 6

Identification: Right-hand-drive version of flagship of Alfa Romeo range competing in executive-car market and featuring 2½-litre engine with automatic transmission.

Engine: Front-mounted V-6-cylinder with belt-driven overhead camshafts and six Dellorto carburettors. Bore × stroke 88 × 68.3 mm, displacement 2492 cc. Output 118 kW (158 bhp) @ 5600 rpm, torque 220 Nm (162 lb ft) @ 4000 rpm.

Transmission: Three-speed automatic transmission. Rear-wheel drive.

Suspension: Front, independent with parallel links, torsion bars, telescopic shock absorbers and anti-roll bar. Rear, de Dion axle with Watt linkage, coil springs, telescopic shock absorbers and anti-roll bar.

Steering: Rack and pinion, power-assisted.

Brakes: Ventilated discs front, discs rear, servo-assisted.

Tyres: 195/70 HR–14.

Dimensions: Length 4760 mm (187.4 in), width 1684 mm (66.3 in), height 1394 mm (54.9 in), wheelbase 2600 mm (102.4 in).

Unladen weight: 1430 kg (3152 lb).

Notes: Standard equipment includes alloy wheels, electric window lifts, central door locking, electrically operated driver's seat-height adjustment and remote-control rear-view mirrors.

ASTON MARTIN (GB)   V8

Identification: Standard model in range of high-performance two-door coupes and convertibles with detail specification improvements.

Engine: Front-mounted V-8-cylinder with twin chain-driven overhead camshafts per cylinder bank and four twin-choke Weber carburettors. Bore × stroke 100 × 85 mm, displacement 5340 cc. Output and torque undisclosed.

Transmission: Single-dry-plate clutch and five-speed manual gearbox or three-speed automatic transmission. Rear-wheel drive.

Suspension: Front, independent with wishbones, coil springs, telescopic shock absorbers and anti-roll bar. Rear, de Dion axle with trailing arms, Watt linkage, coil springs and telescopic shock absorbers.

Steering: Rack and pinion, power-assisted.

Brakes: Ventilated discs front and rear, servo-assisted.

Tyres: GR70 VR-15.

Dimensions: Length 4667 mm (183.8 in), width 1829 mm (72 in), height 1327 mm (52.2 in), wheelbase 2611 mm (102.8 in).

Unladen weight: 1750 kg (3858 lb).

Notes: Standard equipment includes air-conditioning, hide upholstery, electric window lifts, alloy wheels and tinted glass.

ASTON MARTIN (GB)   Lagonda

Identification: Advanced-specification four-door saloon with comprehensive equipment and based on Aston Martin mechanical units and running gear.

Engine: Front-mounted V-8-cylinder with twin chain-driven overhead camshafts per cylinder bank and four twin-choke Weber carburettors. Bore × stroke 100 × 85 mm, displacement 5340 cc. Output and torque undisclosed.

Transmission: Single-dry-plate clutch and three-speed automatic transmission. Rear-wheel drive.

Suspension: Front, independent with wishbones, coil springs, telescopic shock absorbers and anti-roll bar. Rear, de Dion axle with trailing arms, Watt linkage, coil springs and telescopic shock absorbers. Self-levelling.

Steering: Rack and pinion, power-assisted.

Brakes: Ventilated discs front and rear, servo-assisted.

Tyres: 235/70 HR–15.

Dimensions: Length 5283 mm (208 in), width 1816 mm (71.5 in), height 1302 mm (51.3 in), wheelbase 2915 mm (114.8 in).

Unladen weight: 2064 kg (4550 lb).

Notes: Standard equipment includes air-conditioning, dual halogen headlamps, hide upholstery, power-adjustable front seats, electric window lifts and tinted glass.

AUDI (D)

Identification: Intermediate model in range of four-door saloons bridging gap between lower-powered 80 LS and higher-powered fuel-injected GLE versions.

Engine: Front-mounted four-cylinder in-line with belt-driven overhead camshaft and Solex carburettor. Bore × stroke 79.5 × 80 mm, displacement 1588 cc. Output 64 kW (85 bhp) @ 5600 rpm, torque 120 Nm (87 lb ft) @ 3200 rpm.

Transmission: Single-dry-plate clutch and four-speed manual gearbox, three-speed automatic transmission optional extra. Front-wheel drive.

Suspension: Front, independent with MacPherson struts, coil springs, telescopic shock absorbers and anti-roll bar. Rear, dead axle with radius arms, Panhard rod, coil springs and telescopic shock absorbers.

Steering: Rack and pinion.

Brakes: Discs front, drums rear, servo-assisted.

Tyres: 175/70 SR–13.

Dimensions: Length 4433 mm (174.5 in), width 1682 mm (66.2 in), height 1365 mm (53.7 in), wheelbase 2541 mm (100 in).

Unladen weight: 950 kg (2094 lb).

Notes: Standard equipment includes fabric upholstery, head restraints, auxiliary lamps and headlamp washers.

Identification: Additional model to Audi range combining Quattro two-door bodyshell and 1.9-litre version of five-cylinder petrol engine with 80 floor pan.

Engine: Front-mounted five-cylinder in-line with belt-driven overhead camshaft and Zenith carburettor. Bore × stroke 79.5 × 77.4 mm, displacement 1921 cc. Output 86 kW (115 bhp) @ 5900 rpm, torque 155 Nm (114 lb ft) @ 3700 rpm.

Transmission: Single-dry-plate clutch and five-speed manual gearbox, three-speed automatic transmission optional extra. Front-wheel drive.

Suspension: Front, independent with MacPherson struts, coil springs, telescopic shock absorbers and anti-roll bar. Rear, semi-independent with trailing arms, coil springs, Panhard rod and telescopic shock absorbers.

Steering: Rack and pinion, power assistance optional extra.

Brakes: Discs front, drums rear, servo-assisted.

Tyres: 175/70 HR–13.

Dimensions: Length 4348 mm (171.2 in), width 1681 mm (66.2 in), height 1350 mm (53.1 in), wheelbase 2542 mm (100.1 in).

Unladen weight: 1022 kg (2252 lb).

Notes: Standard equipment includes tweed-trimmed upholstery, tinted glass, front and rear spoilers, and alloy wheels.

AUDI (D)

100 Avant L5D

Identification: Diesel-engined addition to Avant range with same trim and equipment specification as petrol-engined 100 L5S.

Engine: Front-mounted four-cylinder in-line with belt-driven overhead camshaft and Bosch diesel injection. Bore × stroke 76.5 × 86.4 mm, displacement 1986 cc. Output 51 kW (70 bhp) @ 4800 rpm, torque 126 Nm (90 lb ft) @ 3000 rpm.

Transmission: Single-dry-plate clutch and four-speed manual gearbox. Front-wheel drive.

Suspension: Front, independent with MacPherson struts, coil springs, telescopic shock absorbers and anti-roll bar. Rear, dead axle with trailing arms, coil springs, Panhard rod, telescopic shock absorbers and anti-roll bar.

Steering: Rack and pinion, power-assisted.

Brakes: Discs front, drums rear, servo-assisted.

Tyres: 165 SR–14.

Dimensions: Length 4610 mm (181.5 in), width 1768 mm (69.6 in), height 1393 mm (54.8 in), wheelbase 2677 mm (105.4 in).

Unladen weight: 1210 kg (2667 lb).

Notes: Standard equipment includes folding rear seat, cloth upholstery, reversing lamps and twin tailgate support struts.

AUDI (D)   200 5T

Identification: New flagship of Audi range combining turbo-charged version of five-cylinder petrol engine with highest level of specification offered in 100-series models.

Engine: Front-mounted five-cylinder in-line with belt-driven overhead camshaft, exhaust-driven turbocharger and Bosch K-Jetronic fuel injection. Bore × stroke 79.5 × 86.4 mm, displacement 2144 cc. Output 125 kW (170 bhp) @ 5300 rpm, torque 273 Nm (195 lb ft) @ 3300 rpm.

Transmission: Single-dry-plate clutch and five-speed manual gearbox or three-speed automatic transmission. Front-wheel drive.

Suspension: Front, independent with MacPherson struts, coil springs, telescopic shock absorbers and anti-roll bar. Rear, dead axle with trailing arms, coil springs, Panhard rod, telescopic shock absorbers and anti-roll bar.

Steering: Rack and pinion, power-assisted.

Brakes: Ventilated discs front, discs rear, servo-assisted.

Tyres: 205/60 HR–15.

Dimensions: Length 4680 mm (184.3 in), width 1768 mm (69.6 in), height 1393 mm (54.8 in), wheelbase 2677 mm (105.4 in).

Unladen weight: 1320 kg (2909 lb).

Notes: Standard equipment includes stereo radio/cassette player, electrically operated sliding roof, electric window lifts, central door locking and cruise control.

AUDI (D) Quattro

Identification: High-performance turbocharged four-wheel-drive two-door four-seater coupe based on Audi 80 floor pan and developed for homologation into competition car.

Engine: Front-mounted five-cylinder in-line with belt-driven overhead camshaft, Bosch K-Jetronic fuel injection and KKK exhaust-driven turbocharger. Bore × stroke 79.5 × 86.4 mm, displacement 2144 cc. Output 150 kW (200 bhp) @ 5500 rpm, torque 285 Nm (210 lb ft) @ 3500 rpm.

Transmission: Single-dry-plate clutch and five-speed manual gearbox. Four-wheel drive.

Suspension: Front, independent with MacPherson struts, coil springs, telescopic shock absorbers and anti-roll bar. Rear, independent with trailing links, MacPherson struts, coil springs, telescopic shock absorbers and anti-roll bar.

Steering: Rack and pinion, power-assisted.

Brakes: Ventilated discs front, discs rear, servo-assisted.

Tyres: 205/60 VR–15.

Dimensions: Length 4404 mm (173.4 in), width 1723 mm (67.8 in), height 1344 mm (52.9 in), wheelbase 2524 mm (99.4 in).

Unladen weight: 1290 kg (2843 lb).

Notes: Standard equipment includes fabric upholstery, full interior trim, height-adjustable driver's seat, front and rear head restraints and five safety belts.

AUSTIN (GB)   Mini Metro 1.0 L

Identification: Intermediate model in 1-litre Metro range bridging gap between base model and higher-geared and more comprehensively equipped HLE economy version.

Engine: Front and transverse-mounted four-cylinder in-line with pushrod-operated overhead valves and SU carburettor. Bore × stroke 64.6 × 76.2 mm, displacement 998 cc. Output 33 kW (44 bhp) @ 5250 rpm, torque 70 Nm (52 lb ft) @ 3000 rpm.

Transmission: Single-dry-plate clutch and four-speed manual gearbox. Front-wheel drive.

Suspension: Front, independent with transverse links, Hydragas units, telescopic shock absorbers and anti-roll bar. Rear, independent with trailing arms, Hydragas units with integral coil springs and dampers and transverse link.

Steering: Rack and pinion.

Brakes: Discs front, drums rear.

Tyres: 135 × 12.

Dimensions: Length 3405 mm (134.1 in), width 1549 mm (60.9 in), height 1361 mm (53.6 in), wheelbase 2251 mm (88.6 in).

Unladen weight: 743 kg (1638 lb).

Notes: Standard equipment includes rear screen wash/wipe, laminated screen, asymmetric-split folding rear seat, reclining front seats and front door stowage bins.

AUSTIN (GB)   Mini Metro 1.3 HLS

Identification: Top model in 1.3-litre Metro range, supplementing 1.3 S with higher level of interior equipment and trim.

Engine: Front and transverse-mounted four-cylinder in-line with pushrod-operated overhead valves and SU carburettor. Bore × stroke 70.6 × 81.3 mm, displacement 1275 cc. Output 47 kW (63 bhp) @ 5650 rpm, torque 98 Nm (72 lb ft) @ 3100 rpm.

Transmission: Single-dry-plate clutch and four-speed manual gearbox. Front-wheel drive.

Suspension: Front, independent with transverse links, Hydragas units, telescopic shock absorbers and anti-roll bar. Rear, independent with trailing arms, Hydragas units with integral coil springs and dampers and transverse link.

Steering: Rack and pinion.

Brakes: Discs front, drums rear, servo-assisted.

Tyres: 155/70 SR–12.

Dimensions: Length 3405 mm (134.1 in), width 1549 mm (60.9 in), height 1361 mm (53.6 in), wheelbase 2251 mm (88.6 in).

Unladen weight: 769 kg (1695 lb).

Notes: Standard equipment includes tinted glass, velour upholstery and door trim, passenger door mirror, carpeted load space, head restraints, wheel trims and cloth headlining.

AUSTIN (GB)   Allegro 1.7 HL

Identification: Top-specification and largest-engined model in Allegro saloon range, supplementing 1.1, 1.3 and 1.5-litre models in standard, L and HL trim.

Engine: Front and transverse-mounted four-cylinder in-line with chain-driven overhead camshaft and twin SU carburettors. Bore × stroke 76.2 × 95.8 mm, displacement 1748 cc. Output 67 kW (90 bhp) @ 5500 rpm, torque 140 Nm (103 lb ft) @ 3100 rpm.

Transmission: Single-dry-plate clutch and five-speed manual gearbox, four-speed automatic transmission optional extra. Front-wheel drive.

Suspension: Front, independent with wishbones, Hydragas spring units with integral shock absorbers. Rear, independent with trailing arms, Hydragas spring units (linked to front units) with integral shock absorbers.

Steering: Rack and pinion.

Brakes: Discs front, drums rear, servo-assisted.

Tyres: 155 SR–13.

Dimensions: Length 3908 mm (153.9 in), width 1613 mm (63.5 in), height 1393 mm (54.8 in), wheelbase 2442 mm (96.1 in).

Unladen weight: 897 kg (1976 lb).

Notes: Standard equipment includes dual headlamps, twin fog lamps, twin exterior mirrors and tinted glass.

AUSTIN (GB)

Maxi 2 HLS

Identification: Revised version of Maxi 1750 with improved specification including new grille, bumpers and hub caps, also available in L and HL forms.

Engine: Front and transverse-mounted four-cylinder in-line with chain-driven overhead camshaft and twin SU carburettors. Bore × stroke 76.2 × 95.8 mm, displacement 1748 cc. Output 68 kW (91 bhp) @ 5250 rpm, torque 144 Nrn (104 lb ft) @ 3400 rpm.

Transmission: Single-dry-plate clutch and five-speed manual gearbox, four-speed automatic transmission optional extra. Front-wheel drive.

Suspension: Front, independent with wishbones, Hydragas spring units with integral shock absorbers. Rear, independent with trailing arms, Hydragas spring units (linked to front units) with integral shock absorbers.

Steering: Rack and pinion.

Brakes: Discs front, drums rear, servo-assisted.

Tyres: 165 SR–13.

Dimensions: Length 4039 mm (159 in), width 1626 mm (64 in), height 1412 mm (55.6 in), wheelbase 2664 mm (104.9 in).

Unladen weight: 1005 kg (2216 lb).

Notes: Standard equipment includes pushbutton radio, four-spoke steering wheel, intermittent screen wipe facility and fabric upholstery.

BENTLEY (GB) Mulsanne

Identification: Replacement model for Bentley T2 four-door saloon incorporating completely restyled bodywork and revised rear suspension from Corniche models.

Engine: Front-mounted V-8-cylinder with pushrod-operated overhead valves and twin SU carburettors. Bore × stroke 104.1 × 99.1 mm, displacement 6750 cc. Output and torque undisclosed.

Transmission: Three-speed automatic transmission. Rear-wheel drive.

Suspension: Front, independent with wishbones, coil springs, telescopic shock absorbers and anti-roll bar. Rear, independent with trailing arms, coil springs, auxiliary gas springs, strut-type shock absorbers and anti-roll bar. Self-levelling.

Steering: Rack and pinion, power-assisted.

Brakes: Ventilated discs front, discs rear, power-assisted.

Tyres: 235/70 HR–15.

Dimensions: Length 5309 mm (209 in), width 1887 mm (74.3 in), height 1485 mm (58.5 in), wheelbase 3061 mm (120.5 in).

Unladen weight: 2245 kg (4948 lb).

Notes: Standard equipment includes air-conditioning, headlamp wash/wipe, electrically operated gear selection, front seat adjustment, windows, mirrors, central door and boot locking, fuel-filler flap and aerial and stereo radio/cassette player with four speakers.

Identification: Larger-engined version of 316 saloon, replacing 1.6-litre model and supplementing 320 and 323i version of 3-series range.

Engine: Front-mounted four-cylinder in-line with belt-driven overhead camshaft and Solex carburettor. Bore × stroke 89.0 × 71.0 mm, displacement 1766 cc. Output 67 kW (90 bhp) @ 5500 rpm, torque 142 Nm (105 lb ft) @ 3500 rpm.

Transmission: Single-dry-plate clutch and four-speed manual gearbox, five-speed gearbox or three-speed automatic transmission optional extra. Rear-wheel drive.

Suspension: Front, independent with MacPherson struts, coil springs, telescopic shock absorbers and anti-roll bar. Rear, independent with trailing arms, coil springs and telescopic shock absorbers.

Steering: Rack and pinion.

Brakes: Discs front, drums rear, servo-assisted.

Tyres: 165 SR–13.

Dimensions: Length 4350 mm (171.3 in), width 1610 mm (63.4 in), height 1380 mm (54.3 in), wheelbase 2560 mm (100.8 in).

Unladen weight: 1020 kg (2249 lb).

Notes: Standard equipment includes fabric upholstery, halogen headlamps and transistorized ignition.

BMW (D)   323i

Identification: Improved version of top model in 3-series range incorporating new upholstery, door linings, carpets and head restraints and new interior trim colours.

Engine: Front-mounted six-cylinder in-line with belt-driven overhead camshaft and Bosch fuel injection. Bore × stroke 80 × 76.8 mm, displacement 2315 cc. Output 105 kW (143 bhp) @ 6000 rpm, torque 190 Nm (140 lb ft) @ 4500 rpm.

Transmission: Single-dry-plate clutch and five-speed manual gearbox. Rear-wheel drive.

Suspension: Front, independent with MacPherson struts, coil springs, telescopic shock absorbers and anti-roll bar. Rear, independent with semi-trailing arms, coil springs and telescopic shock absorbers.

Steering: Rack and pinion, power-assistance optional extra.

Brakes: Discs front, drums rear, servo-assisted.

Tyres: 185/70 HR–13.

Dimensions: Length 4350 mm (171.3 in), width 1610 mm (63.4 in), height 1380 mm (54.3 in), wheelbase 2563 mm (101 in).

Unladen weight: 1135 kg (2502 lb).

Notes: Standard equipment includes dual halogen headlamps and velour upholstery.

Identification: High-specification model in 5-series range of four-door saloons, bridging gap between 520 and 525 models and latest 535i derivative.

Engine: Front-mounted six-cylinder in-line with chain-driven overhead camshaft and Bosch L-Jetronic fuel injection. Bore × stroke 86 × 80 mm, displacement 2788 cc. Output 132 kW (177 bhp) @ 5800 rpm, torque 240 Nm (174 lb ft) @ 4000 rpm.

Transmission: Single-dry-plate clutch and four-speed manual gearbox, overdrive fifth or three-speed automatic transmission optional extra. Rear-wheel drive.

Suspension: Front, independent with MacPherson struts, coil springs, telescopic shock absorbers and anti-roll bar. Rear, independent with trailing arms, coil springs, telescopic shock absorbers and anti-roll bar.

Steering: Worm and roller, power-assisted.

Brakes: Ventilated discs front, discs rear, servo-assisted.

Tyres: 195/70 VR-14.

Dimensions: Length 4620 mm (181.9 in), width 1690 mm (66.5 in), height 1425 mm (56.1 in), wheelbase 2640 mm (103.9 in).

Unladen weight: 1410 kg (3108 lb).

Notes: Standard equipment includes velour upholstery, head restraints, electric window lifts, central door locking and remote-control rear-view mirrors.

BMW (D) M 535i

Identification: Sporting addition to top of 5-series range of saloons incorporating front and rear bodywork spoilers, modified suspension and running gear and competition-orientated seating.

Engine: Front-mounted six-cylinder in-line with chain-driven overhead camshaft and Bosch L-Jetronic fuel injection. Bore × stroke 93.4 × 84 mm, displacement 3453 cc. Output 160 kW (218 bhp) @ 5200 rpm, torque 314 Nm (224 lb ft) @ 4000 rpm.

Transmission: Single-dry-plate clutch and five-speed manual gearbox. Rear-wheel drive.

Suspension: Front, independent with MacPherson struts, coil springs, telescopic shock absorbers and anti-roll bar. Rear, independent with semi-trailing arms, coil springs, telescopic shock absorbers and anti-roll bar.

Steering: Recirculating ball, power-assisted.

Brakes: Ventilated discs front and rear, servo-assisted.

Tyres: 195/70 VR–14.

Dimensions: Length 4623 mm (182 in), width 1692 mm (66.6 in), height 1422 mm (56 in), wheelbase 2639 mm (103.9 in).

Unladen weight: 1430 kg (3152 lb).

Notes: Standard equipment includes Recaro front seats, sports steering wheel and protective side body mouldings.

Identification: New flagship of BMW 7-series range powered by turbocharged version of six-cylinder engine fitted to 732i saloon.

Engine: Front-mounted six-cylinder in-line with chain-driven overhead camshaft, exhaust-driven turbocharger and Bosch L-Jetronic fuel injection. Bore × stroke 89 × 86 mm, displacement 3210 cc. Output 185 kW (252 bhp) @ 5500 rpm, torque 380 Nm (280 lb ft) @ 2600 rpm.

Transmission: Three-speed automatic transmission. Rear-wheel drive.

Suspension: Front, independent with MacPherson struts, coil springs, telescopic shock absorbers and anti-roll bar. Rear, independent with trailing arms, coil springs and telescopic shock absorbers.

Steering: Recirculating ball, power-assisted.

Brakes: Ventilated discs front, discs rear, servo-assisted.

Tyres: 205/70 VR–14.

Dimensions: Length 4860 mm (191.3 in), width 1800 mm (70.9 in), height 1430 mm (56.3 in), wheelbase 2795 mm (110 in).

Unladen weight: 1610 kg (3550 lb).

Notes: Standard equipment includes ABS anti-lock braking, heated exterior mirror and door lock and 12-function on-board computer monitoring time, distance, speed, temperature and consumption.

BRISTOL (GB)   412/S3 Beaufighter

Identification: Four-seater coupe developed from 412/S2 and incorporating turbocharged engine and restyled upper bodywork with removable glass roof panel and dual headlamps.

Engine: Front-mounted V-8-cylinder with pushrod-operated overhead valves, exhaust-driven turbocharger and Carter carburettor. Bore × stroke 101.6 × 90.9 mm, displacement 5898 cc. Output and torque undisclosed.

Transmission: Three-speed automatic transmission. Rear-wheel drive.

Suspension: Front, independent with wishbones, coil springs, adjustable telescopic shock absorbers and anti-roll bar. Rear, live axle with Watt linkage, torsion bars and adjustable telescopic shock absorbers.

Steering: Recirculating ball, power-assisted.

Brakes: Discs front and rear, servo-assisted.

Tyres: 225/70 VR-15.

Dimensions: Length 4940 mm (194.5 in), width 1765 mm (69.5 in), height 1435 mm (56.5 in), wheelbase 2896 mm (114 in).

Unladen weight: 1760 kg (3880 lb).

Notes: Standard equipment includes electrically adjustable seats, removable rear roof section, leather upholstery and automatic door locking.

BUICK (USA)   Skylark Limited

Identification: High-specification four-door saloon version of Skylark based on GM X-car design and incorporating minor styling changes and interior improvements.

Engine: Front and transverse-mounted four-cylinder in-line with pushrod-operated overhead valves and Rochester carburettor. Bore × stroke 101.6 × 76.2 mm, displacement 2474 cc. Output 67 kW (90 bhp) @ 4000 rpm, torque 185 Nm (134 lb ft) @ 2400 rpm.

Transmission: Single-dry-plate clutch and four-speed manual overdrive gearbox, three-speed automatic transmission optional extra. Front-wheel drive.

Suspension: Front, independent with MacPherson struts, coil springs, telescopic shock absorbers and anti-roll bar. Rear, live axle with trailing arms, Panhard rod, coil springs and telescopic shock absorbers.

Steering: Rack and pinion, power-assistance optional extra.

Brakes: Discs front, drums rear, servo-assisted.

Tyres: 185/80 SR–13.

Dimensions: Length 4599 mm (181.1 in), width 1716 mm (67.6 in), height 1315 mm (51.8 in), wheelbase 2664 mm (104.9 in).

Unladen weight: 1180 kg (2600 lb).

Notes: Standard equipment includes centre console, cruise control and 'wet arm' windscreen wiping system.

CADILLAC (USA)   Seville

Identification: Improved version of smaller-bodied Cadillac saloon featuring diesel engine as standard equipment but with option of 6-litre fuel-injected petrol engine utilizing four, six or eight cylinders according to conditions.

Engine: Front-mounted V-8-cylinder with pushrod-operated overhead valves and GM diesel fuel injection. Bore × stroke 103.1 × 86 mm, displacement 5729 cc. Output 104 kW (140 bhp) @ 3800 rpm, torque 359 Nm (265 lb ft) @ 1400 rpm.

Transmission: Three-speed automatic transmission. Front-wheel drive.

Suspension: Front, independent with wishbones, coil springs, telescopic shock absorbers and anti-roll bar. Rear, independent with semi-elliptic springs, telescopic shock absorbers and anti-roll bar. Self-levelling.

Steering: Recirculating ball, power-assisted.

Brakes: Discs front and rear, servo-assisted.

Tyres: 225/70 VR–15.

Dimensions: Length 5202 mm (204.8 in), width 1801 mm (70.9 in), height 1378 mm (54.3 in), wheelbase 2895 mm (114 in).

Unladen weight: 1890 kg (4167 lb).

Notes: Standard equipment includes fabric upholstery, divided front seat, electronic climate control, front spoiler and simulated teak instrument panel.

CHEVROLET (USA)   Citation

Identification: Improved Chevrolet version of GM X-car incorporating styling changes including new grille and also available as three-door hatchback coupe.

Engine: Front and transverse-mounted four-cylinder in-line with pushrod-operated overhead valves and Rochester carburettor. Bore × stroke 101.6 × 76.2 mm, displacement 2474 cc. Output 67 kW (90 bhp) @ 4000 rpm, torque 185 Nm (134 lb ft) @ 2400 rpm.

Transmission: Single-dry-plate clutch and four-speed manual gearbox, three-speed automatic transmission optional extra. Front-wheel drive.

Suspension: Front, independent with MacPherson struts, coil springs, telescopic shock absorbers and anti-roll bar. Rear, dead axle with trailing arms, Panhard rod, coil springs and telescopic shock absorbers.

Steering: Rack and pinion, power-assistance optional extra.

Brakes: Discs front, drums rear, servo-assisted.

Tyres: 185/80 SR–13.

Dimensions: Length 4488 mm (176.7 in), width 1735 mm (68.3 in), height 1392 mm (54.8 in), wheelbase 2664 mm (104.9 in).

Unladen weight: 1180 kg (2600 lb).

Notes: Standard equipment includes individual front seats with integral head restraints, centre console, bumper overriders and front air dam.

CITROEN (F)   Visa Super

Identification: Larger-engined version of new five-door hatchback supplementing 652 cc twin-cylinder air-cooled-engined Special and Club models.

Engine: Front and transverse-mounted four-cylinder in-line with chain-driven overhead camshaft and Solex carburettor. Bore × stroke 72 × 69 mm, displacement 1124 cc. Output 42 kW (57 bhp) @ 6250 rpm, torque 83 Nm (59 lb ft) @ 3000 rpm.

Transmission: Single-dry-plate clutch and four-speed manual gearbox. Front-wheel drive.

Suspension: Front, independent with MacPherson struts, coil springs, telescopic shock absorbers and anti-roll bar. Rear, independent with trailing arms, coil springs, telescopic shock absorbers and anti-roll bar.

Steering: Rack and pinion.

Brakes: Discs front, drums rear.

Tyres: 145 SR–13.

Dimensions: Length 3721 mm (146.5 in), width 1537 mm (60.5 in), height 1417 mm (55.8 in), wheelbase 2419 mm (95.3 in).

Unladen weight: 800 kg (1764 lb).

Notes: Standard equipment includes folding rear seat, rear fog lamps and rear screen wash/wipe.

CITROEN (F)   GSA Club Estate

Identification: Five-door estate car developed from GS model and incorporating similar interior and exterior trim to that fitted to GSA Club saloon.

Engine: Front-mounted air-cooled four-cylinder horizontally opposed with belt-driven overhead camshafts and Weber carburettor. Bore × stroke 79.4 × 65.6 mm, displacement 1299 cc. Output 48 kW (65 bhp) @ 5500 rpm, torque 101 Nm (72 lb ft) @ 3500 rpm.

Transmission: Single-dry-plate clutch and four-speed manual gearbox, three-speed semi-automatic transmission optional extra. Front-wheel drive.

Suspension: Front, independent with wishbones, hydropneumatic units and anti-roll bar. Rear, independent with trailing arms, hydropneumatic units and anti-roll bar. Self-levelling front and rear.

Steering: Rack and pinion.

Brakes: Discs front and rear, power-assisted.

Tyres: 145 SR–15.

Dimensions: Length 4156 mm (163.6 in), width 1626 mm (64 in), height 1349 mm (53.1 in), wheelbase 2550 mm (100.4 in).

Unladen weight: 965 kg (2127 lb).

Notes: Standard equipment includes folding rear seat, reversing lamps and rear fog lamps, halogen headlamps and cloth upholstery.

CITROEN (F)   GSA Pallas

Identification: Top model in revised GSA range of five-door saloons and estate cars developed from GS series and incorporating styling changes and improved interior.

Engine: Front-mounted air-cooled four-cylinder horizontally opposed with belt-driven overhead camshafts and Weber carburettor. Bore × stroke 79.4 × 65.6 mm, displacement 1299 cc. Output 48 kW (65 bhp) @ 5500 rpm, torque 101 Nm (72 lb ft) @ 3500 rpm.

Transmission: Single-dry-plate clutch and five-speed manual gearbox, three-speed semi-automatic transmission optional extra. Front-wheel drive.

Suspension: Front, independent with wishbones, hydropneumatic units and anti-roll bar. Rear, independent with trailing arms, hydropneumatic units and anti-roll bar. Self-levelling front and rear.

Steering: Rack and pinion.

Brakes: Discs front and rear, power-assisted.

Tyres: 145 SR–15.

Dimensions: Length 4195 mm (165.2 in), width 1626 mm (64 in), height 1349 mm (53.1 in), wheelbase 2550 mm (100.4 in).

Unladen weight: 955 kg (2105 lb).

Notes: Standard equipment includes head restraints, remote-controlled exterior mirror, chromed wheel trims and folding rear seat.

CITROEN (F)　　　　CX 2400 Prestige auto

Identification: Automatic-transmission version of most luxurious model in CX range of saloons and estate cars, also available with five-speed manual gearbox.

Engine: Front and transverse-mounted four-cylinder in-line with pushrod-operated overhead valves and Bosch-L-Jetronic fuel injection. Bore × stroke 93.5 × 85.5 mm, displacement 2347 cc. Output 96 kW (128 bhp) @ 4800 rpm, torque 201 Nm (145 lb ft) @ 3600 rpm.

Transmission: Three-speed automatic transmission or five-speed manual gearbox. Front-wheel drive.

Suspension: Front, independent with wishbones, hydropneumatic suspension units and anti-roll bar. Rear, independent with trailing arms, hydropneumatic suspension units and anti-roll bar. Self-levelling.

Steering: Rack and pinion, power-assisted.

Brakes: Discs front and rear, power-assisted.

Tyres: 185 HR–14.

Dimensions: Length 4915 mm (193.5 in), width 1734 mm (68.3 in), height 1397 mm (55 in), wheelbase 3099 mm (122 in).

Unladen weight: 1455 kg (3207 lb).

Notes: Standard equipment includes air-conditioning, tinted glass, electric window lifts, central locking, vinyl roof, fabric upholstery and rear passenger foot rests.

COLT (J)   Lancer 1400 GLX

Identification: Smaller-engined of two completely restyled Lancer saloons supplementing 1600 GSR with 1.6-litre balancer engine.

Engine: Front-mounted four-cylinder in-line with belt-driven overhead camshaft and Solex carburettor. Bore × stroke 74 × 82 mm, displacement 1410 cc. Output 50 kW (68 bhp) @ 5000 rpm, torque 105 Nm (75 lb ft) @ 3500 rpm.

Transmission: Single-dry-plate clutch and four-speed manual gearbox. Rear-wheel drive.

Suspension: Front, independent with MacPherson struts, coil springs, telescopic shock absorbers and anti-roll bar. Rear, live axle with four links, coil springs, telescopic shock absorbers and anti-roll bar.

Steering: Recirculating ball.

Brakes: Discs front, drums rear, servo-assisted.

Tyres: 155 SR–13.

Dimensions: Length 4225 mm (166.3 in), width 1620 mm (63.8 in), height 1385 mm (54.5 in), wheelbase 2440 mm (88.2 in).

Unladen weight: 935 kg (2061 lb).

Notes: Standard equipment includes adjustable steering column, halogen headlamps, transistorized ignition and three-speed wash/wipe system.

COLT (J)

Lancer 1600 GSR

Identification: More powerful version of restyled Lancer four-door saloon featuring Saturn 80 balancer engine and five-speed transmission.

Engine: Front-mounted four-cylinder in-line with belt-driven overhead camshaft and twin Solex carburettors. Bore × stroke 76.9 × 86 mm, displacement 1597 cc. Output 60 kW (82 bhp) @ 5500 rpm, torque 116 Nm (83 lb ft) @ 3500 rpm.

Transmission: Single-dry-plate clutch and five-speed manual gearbox. Rear-wheel drive.

Suspension: Front, independent with MacPherson struts, coil springs, telescopic shock absorbers and anti-roll bar. Rear, live axle with four links, coil springs, telescopic shock absorbers and anti-roll bar.

Steering: Recirculating ball.

Brakes: Discs front, drums rear, servo-assisted.

Tyres: 165 SR–13.

Dimensions: Length 4225 mm (166.3 in), width 1620 mm (63.8 in), height 1385 mm (54.5 in), wheelbase 2440 mm (88.2 in).

Unladen weight: 975 kg (2149 lb).

Notes: Standard equipment includes quartz digital clock, illuminated speedometer needle, adjustable steering column, halogen headlamps and three-speed wash/wipe system.

COLT (J) Galant 2000

Identification: Restyled four-door saloon with new 2-litre engine, also available with 1.6-litre engine and four-speed gearbox.

Engine: Front-mounted four-cylinder in-line with belt-driven overhead camshaft and Mikuni-Solex carburettor. Bore × stroke 85 × 88 mm, displacement 1997 cc. Output 76 kW (102 bhp) @ 5500 rpm, torque 152 Nm (112 lb ft) @ 3500 rpm.

Transmission: Single-dry-plate clutch and five-speed manual gearbox, three-speed automatic transmission optional extra. Rear-wheel drive.

Suspension: Front, independent with MacPherson struts, coil springs, telescopic shock absorbers and anti-roll bar. Rear, independent with trailing arms, lateral links, coil springs and telescopic shock absorbers.

Steering: Recirculating ball, power-assisted.

Brakes: Discs front and rear, servo-assisted.

Tyres: 165 SR–14.

Dimensions: Length 4470 mm (176 in), width 1680 mm (66.1 in), height 1370 mm (53.9 in), wheelbase 2530 mm (99.6 in).

Unladen weight: 1170 kg (2579 lb).

Notes: Standard equipment includes alloy wheels, height-adjustable driver's seat and steering wheel, electric window lifts and headlamp wash/wipe.

COLT (J)

Identification: Revised version of two-door four-seater coupe with new 2-litre engine and changes to front and rear styling and interior equipment.

Engine: Front-mounted four-cylinder in-line with belt-driven overhead camshaft and twin Mikuni-Solex carburettors. Bore × stroke 85 × 88 mm, displacement 1997 cc. Output 76 kW (102 bhp) @ 5500 rpm, torque 152 Nm (112 lb ft) @ 3500 rpm.

Transmission: Single-dry-plate clutch and five-speed manual gearbox. Rear-wheel drive.

Suspension: Front, independent with MacPherson struts, coil springs, telescopic shock absorbers and anti-roll bar. Rear, independent with trailing arms, lateral links, coil springs and telescopic shock absorbers.

Steering: Recirculating ball, power-assisted.

Brakes: Discs front, drums rear, servo-assisted.

Tyres: 195/70 HR–14.

Dimensions: Length 4525 mm (178.2 in), width 1675 mm (66 in), height 1355 mm (53.4 in), wheelbase 2530 mm (99.6 in).

Unladen weight: 1220 kg (2689 lb).

Notes:- Standard equipment includes alloy wheels, electric window lifts, headlamp wash/wipe, stereo radio/cassette player and internally adjustable rear-view mirrors.

DAIMLER (GB)

5.3 Vanden Plas

Identification: Latest version of top model in Daimler saloon range with more powerful and more economical V-12 engine incorporating electronic digital fuel injection.

Engine: Front-mounted V-12-cylinder with single belt-driven overhead camshafts and Lucas-Bosch electronic digital fuel injection. Bore × stroke 90 × 70 mm, displacement 5343 cc. Output 224 kW (300 bhp) @ 5400 rpm, torque 432 Nm (318 lb ft) @ 3900 rpm.

Transmission: Three-speed automatic transmission. Rear-wheel drive.

Suspension: Front, independent with wishbones, coil springs, telescopic shock absorbers and anti-roll bar. Rear, independent with trailing arms, wishbones, fixed drive shafts, dual coil springs and telescopic shock absorbers.

Steering: Rack and pinion, power-assisted.

Brakes: Discs front and rear, servo-assisted.

Tyres: 205/70 VR–15.

Dimensions: Length 4959 mm (195.2 in), width 1770 mm (69.7 in), height 1377 mm (54 in), wheelbase 2866 mm (112.8 in).

Unladen weight: 1885 kg (4155 lb).

Notes: Standard equipment includes air-conditioning, stereo radio/cassette player, hide upholstery and limited-slip differential.

DATSUN (J)   Cherry 5-door Hatchback

Identification: Additional model to restyled Cherry range, supplementing three-door hatchback and powered by 1.1-litre engine also used for Cherry coupe.

Engine: Front and transverse-mounted four-cylinder in-line with pushrod-operated overhead valves and Hitachi carburettor. Bore × stroke 73 × 70 mm, displacement 1171 cc. Output 38 kW (52 bhp) @ 5600 rpm, torque 80 Nm (57 lb ft) @ 3600 rpm.

Transmission: Single-dry-plate clutch and four-speed manual gearbox. Front-wheel drive.

Suspension: Front, independent with MacPherson struts, trailing arms, coil springs and telescopic shock absorbers. Rear, independent with trailing arms, coil springs and telescopic shock absorbers.

Steering: Rack and pinion.

Brakes: Discs front, drums rear, servo-assisted.

Tyres: 155 SR–13.

Dimensions: Length 3889 mm (153.1 in), width 1620 mm (63.8 in), height 1359 mm (53.5 in), wheelbase 2395 mm (94.3 in).

Unladen weight: 790 kg (1741 lb).

Notes: Standard equipment includes radio, cloth upholstery, quartz clock, tinted glass and halogen headlamps.

DATSUN (J)   Sunny 1.2 GL 4-door

Identification: Four-door version of facelifted new Sunny range of saloons, coupe and conventional and fastback estate cars with choice of 1.2-litre and 1.4-litre engines.

Engine: Front-mounted four-cylinder in-line with pushrod-operated overhead valves and Hitachi carburettor. Bore × stroke 73 × 70 mm, displacement 1171 cc. Output 39 kW (52 bhp) @ 5600 rpm, torque 81 Nm (59 lb ft) @ 4000 rpm.

Transmission: Single-dry-plate clutch and four-speed manual gearbox. Rear-wheel drive.

Suspension: Front, independent with MacPherson struts, coil springs, telescopic shock absorbers and anti-roll bar. Rear, live axle with trailing arms, coil springs and telescopic shock absorbers.

Steering: Recirculating ball.

Brakes: Discs front, drums rear, servo-assisted.

Tyres: 155 SR–13.

Dimensions: Length 4000 mm (157.5 in), width 1590 mm (62.6 in), height 1360 mm (53.5 in), wheelbase 2340 mm (92.1 in).

Unladen weight: 830 kg (1830 lb).

Notes: Three-speed automatic transmission optional extra with 1.4-litre engine.

DATSUN (J)   Sunny 1.4 GL Fastback Estate

Identification: Sporting estate version of facelifted new Sunny range incorporating restyled front grille and lamps assembly, and revised front and rear bumpers.

Engine: Front-mounted four-cylinder in-line with pushrod-operated overhead valves and Hitachi carburettor. Bore × stroke 76 × 77 mm, displacement 1397 cc. Output 47 kW (63 bhp) @ 5600 rpm, torque 100 Nm (72 lb ft) @ 3600 rpm.

Transmission: Single-dry-plate clutch and four-speed manual gearbox, three-speed automatic transmission optional extra. Rear-wheel drive.

Suspension: Front, independent with MacPherson struts, coil springs, telescopic shock absorbers and anti-roll bar. Rear, live axle with trailing arms, coil springs and telescopic shock absorbers.

Steering: Recirculating ball.

Brakes: Discs front, drums rear, servo-assisted.

Tyres: 155 SR–13.

Dimensions: Length 4160 mm (163.8 in), width 1580 mm (62.2 in), height 1336 mm (52.6 in), wheelbase 2340 mm (92.1 in).

Unladen weight: 895 kg (1973 lb).

Notes: Standard equipment includes rear screen wash/wipe, tinted glass, carpeted luggage area and individually folding rear seats.

DATSUN (J)　　　　Sunny 1.4 GL Coupe

Identification: Hatchback coupe version of facelifted Sunny range with 1.4-litre engine and choice of four-speed or five-speed gearbox.

Engine: Front-mounted four-cylinder in-line with pushrod-operated overhead valves and Hitachi carburettor. Bore × stroke 76 × 77 mm, displacement 1397 cc. Output 47 kW (63 bhp) @ 5600 rpm, torque 100 Nm (72 lb ft) @ 3600 rpm.

Transmission: Single-dry-plate clutch and four-speed gearbox, five-speed manual gearbox optional extra. Rear-wheel drive.

Suspension: Front, independent with MacPherson struts, coil springs, telescopic shock absorbers and anti-roll bar. Rear, live axle with trailing arms, coil springs and telescopic shock absorbers.

Steering: Recirculating ball.

Brakes: Discs front, drums rear, servo-assisted.

Tyres: 155 SR–13.

Dimensions: Length 4000 mm (157.5 in), width 1590 mm (62.6 in), height 1360 mm (53.5 in), wheelbase 2340 mm (92.1 in).

Unladen weight: 855 kg (1884 lb).

Notes: Standard equipment includes reclining front seats with head restraints, individually folding rear seats and tinted glass.

DATSUN (J)   Violet 140J Saloon

Identification: Saloon version of restyled Violet range, supplementing 1.6-litre-engined model and incorporating revised dashboard and suspension improvements.

Engine: Front-mounted four-cylinder in-line with pushrod-operated overhead valves and Hitachi carburettor. Bore × stroke 76 × 77 mm, displacement 1397 cc. Output 47 kW (63 bhp) @ 5600 rpm, torque 100 Nm (72 lb ft) @ 3600 rpm.

Transmission: Single-dry-plate clutch and four-speed manual gearbox. Rear-wheel drive.

Suspension: Front, independent with MacPherson struts, coil springs, telescopic shock absorbers and anti-roll bar. Rear, live axle with trailing arms, coil springs and telescopic shock absorbers.

Steering: Recirculating ball.

Brakes: Discs front, drums rear, servo-assisted.

Tyres: 165 SR–13.

Dimensions: Length 4220 mm (166.1 in), width 1605 mm (63.2 in), height 1390 mm (54.7 in), wheelbase 2400 mm (94.5 in).

Unladen weight: 880 kg (1940 lb).

Notes: Standard equipment includes halogen headlamps, velour upholstery and interior fuel-filler cover release and luggage compartment release.

DATSUN (J)   Violet 160J Hatchback

Identification: Three-door coupe version of revised Violet range supplementing 1.4-litre and 1.6-litre four-door saloons.

Engine: Front-mounted four-cylinder in-line with chain-driven overhead camshaft and twin Hitachi carburettors. Bore × stroke 83 × 73.7 mm, displacement 1595 cc. Output 64 kW (87 bhp) @ 5800 rpm, torque 127 Nm (91 lb ft) @ 3800 rpm.

Transmission: Single-dry-plate clutch and five-speed manual gearbox. Rear-wheel drive.

Suspension: Front, independent with MacPherson struts, coil springs, telescopic shock absorbers and anti-roll bar. Rear, live axle with trailing arms, coil springs and telescopic shock absorbers.

Steering: Recirculating ball.

Brakes: Discs front, drums rear, servo-assisted.

Tyres: 165 SR–13.

Dimensions: Length 4220 mm (166.1 in), width 1605 mm (63.2 in), height 1350 mm (53.2 in), wheelbase 2400 mm (94.5 in).

Unladen weight: 945 kg (2083 lb).

Notes: Standard equipment includes halogen headlamps, velour upholstery and interior fuel-filler cover release and rear door release.

DATSUN (J)   Bluebird 1.6 Saloon

Identification: Smallest-engined saloon version of range of restyled 1.6-litre and 1.8-litre cars also available with coupe or estate car bodywork.

Engine: Front-mounted four-cylinder in-line with chain-driven overhead camshaft and Nikki carburettor. Bore × stroke 83 × 73.3 mm, displacement 1595 cc. Output 60 kW (81 bhp) @ 5600 rpm, torque 124 Nm (89 lb ft) @ 3600 rpm.

Transmission: Single-dry-plate clutch and four-speed manual gearbox, three-speed automatic transmission optional extra on 1.8-litre saloon. Rear-wheel drive.

Suspension: Front, independent with MacPherson struts, coil springs, telescopic shock absorbers and anti-roll bar. Rear, independent with semi-trailing arms, coil springs, telescopic shock absorbers and anti-roll bar.

Steering: Rack and pinion.

Brakes: Ventilated discs front, drums rear, servo-assisted.

Tyres: 165 SR–14.

Dimensions: Length 4350 mm (171.3 in), width 1656 mm (65.2 in), height 1400 mm (55.1 in), wheelbase 2525 mm (99.4 in).

Unladen weight: 1075 kg (2370 lb).

Notes: Standard equipment includes reclining front seats with head restraints, digital clock with date, remote-control fuel-filler cap and boot lid and door-open warning buzzer.

DATSUN (J)

Bluebird 1.8 Coupe

Identification: Top model in revised Bluebird range with five-speed transmission, uprated engine and wider wheels and tyres.

Engine: Front-mounted four-cylinder in-line with chain-driven overhead camshaft and SU carburettor. Bore × stroke 85 × 78 mm, displacement 1770 cc. Output 66 kW (90 bhp) @ 5800 rpm, torque 141 Nm (100.5 lb ft) @ 3800 rpm.

Transmission: Single-dry-plate clutch and five-speed manual gearbox. Rear-wheel drive.

Suspension: Front, independent with MacPherson struts, coil springs, telescopic shock absorbers and anti-roll bar. Rear, independent with semi-trailing arms, coil springs, telescopic shock absorbers and anti-roll bar.

Steering: Rack and pinion.

Brakes: Ventilated discs front, drums rear, servo-assisted.

Tyres: 185/70 SR–14.

Dimensions: Length 4361 mm (171.7 in), width 1656 mm (65.2 in), height 1384 mm (54.5 in), wheelbase 2525 mm (99.4 in).

Unladen weight: 1100 kg (2425 lb).

Notes: Standard equipment includes alloy wheels, adjustable steering column, reclining front seats with head restraints and door-open warning buzzer.

DATSUN (J) Bluebird 1.8 Estate

Identification: Five-door version of new Bluebird range incorporating improved suspension and steering and more spacious restyled bodywork.

Engine: Front-mounted four-cylinder in-line with chain-driven overhead camshaft and Nikki carburettor. Bore × stroke 85 × 78 mm, displacement 1770 cc. Output 65 kW (88 bhp) @ 5600 rpm, torque 138 Nm (98.3 lb ft) @ 3600 rpm.

Transmission: Single-dry-plate clutch and four-speed manual gearbox. Rear-wheel drive.

Suspension: Front, independent with MacPherson struts, coil springs, telescopic shock absorbers and anti-roll bar. Rear, live axle with semi-elliptic leaf springs and telescopic shock absorbers.

Steering: Rack and pinion.

Brakes: Ventilated discs front, drums rear, servo-assisted.

Tyres: 165 SR–14.

Dimensions: Length 4400 mm (173.2 in), width 1656 mm (65.2 in), height 1405 mm (55.3 in), wheelbase 2525 mm (99.4 in).

Unladen weight: 1120 kg (2469 lb).

Notes: Standard equipment includes reclining front seats with head restraints, rear screen wash/wipe, digital clock with date and door-open warning buzzer.

DATSUN (J)   280C Saloon

Identification: New executive saloon with completely restyled bodywork, revised suspension and more comprehensive standard specification.

Engine: Front-mounted six-cylinder in-line with chain-driven overhead camshaft and Hitachi carburettor. Bore × stroke 86 × 79 mm, displacement 2753 cc. Output 92 kW (125 bhp) @ 4800 rpm, torque 203 Nm (145 lb ft) @ 3200 rpm.

Transmission: Three-speed automatic transmission standard, five-speed manual gearbox to special order with cost reduction. Rear-wheel drive.

Suspension: Front, independent with wishbones, coil springs, telescopic shock absorbers and anti-roll bar. Rear, live axle with trailing arms, coil springs, telescopic shock absorbers and anti-roll bar.

Steering: Recirculating ball, power-assisted.

Brakes: Discs front and rear, servo-assisted.

Tyres: 195/70 HR–14.

Dimensions: Length 4815 mm (189.6 in), width 1715 mm (67.5 in), height 1430 mm (56.3 in), wheelbase 2690 mm (105.9 in).

Unladen weight: 1375 kg (3031 lb).

Notes: Standard equipment includes air-conditioning, alloy wheels, electric window lifts, central door locking and radio/stereo cassette player.

DATSUN (J)

Identification: Seven-seater estate version of new 280C range incorporating rear-facing seat and electrically operated nearside loading window.

Engine: Front-mounted six-cylinder in-line with chain-driven overhead camshaft and Hitachi carburettor. Bore × stroke 86 × 79 mm, displacement 2753 cc. Output 92 kW (125 bhp) @ 4800 rpm, torque 203 Nm (145 lb ft) @ 3200 rpm.

Transmission: Single-dry-plate clutch and five-speed manual gearbox, three-speed automatic transmission optional extra. Rear-wheel drive.

Suspension: Front, independent with wishbones, coil springs, telescopic shock absorbers and anti-roll bar. Rear, live axle with semi-elliptic leaf springs, telescopic shock absorbers and anti-roll bar.

Steering: Recirculating ball, power-assisted.

Brakes: Discs front, drums rear, servo-assisted.

Tyres: 195/70 HR–14.

Dimensions: Length 4750 mm (187 in), width 1715 mm (67.5 in), height 1495 mm (58.9 in), wheelbase 2690 mm (105.9 in).

Unladen weight: 1430 kg (3153 lb).

Notes: Standard equipment includes electric window lifts, headlamp washers, radio/stereo cassette player and adjustable steering wheel.

DE TOMASO (I)   **Pantera GTS**

Identification: Highest-specification version of Pantera two-seater coupe combining 5.8-litre engine, five-speed transmission and limited-slip differential with comprehensive interior equipment.

Engine: Centrally mounted Ford V-8-cylinder with pushrod-operated overhead valves and Ford carburettor. Bore × stroke 101.6 × 88.9 mm, displacement 5763 cc. Output 224 kW (300 bhp) @ 5000 rpm, torque approx. 360 Nm (265 lb ft) @ 3500 rpm.

Transmission: Single-dry-plate clutch and five-speed manual gearbox. Rear-wheel drive.

Suspension: Front, independent with wishbones, coil springs, telescopic shock absorbers and anti-roll bar. Rear, independent with wishbones, coil springs, telescopic shock absorbers and anti-roll bar.

Steering: Rack and pinion.

Brakes: Ventilated discs front and rear, servo-assisted.

Tyres: 185/70 VR–15 front, 215/70 VR–15 rear.

Dimensions: Length 4452 mm (175.3 in), width 1810 mm (71.3 in), height 1100 mm (43.3 in), wheelbase 2515 mm (99 in).

Unladen weight: 1430 kg (3152 lb).

Notes: Standard equipment includes air-conditioning, electronic ignition, electric window lifts, tinted glass and clock.

DE TOMASO (I)   Longchamp

Identification: Latest version of two-door four-seater saloon supplementing Deauville four-door five-seater and featuring coachbuilt steel bodywork.

Engine: Front-mounted Ford V-8-cylinder with pushrod-operated overhead valves and Ford carburettor. Bore × stroke 101.6 × 88.9 mm, displacement 5763 cc. Output 224 kW (300 bhp) @ 5000 rpm, torque approx. 360 Nm (265 lb ft) @ 3500 rpm.

Transmission: Three-speed automatic transmission. Rear-wheel drive.

Suspension: Front, independent with wishbones, coil springs, telescopic shock absorbers and anti-roll bar. Rear, independent with wishbones, dual coil springs and telescopic shock absorbers.

Steering: Rack and pinion, power-assisted.

Brakes: Ventilated discs front and rear, servo-assisted.

Tyres: 215/70 VR–15.

Dimensions: Length 4530 mm (178.4 in), width 1830 mm (72.1 in), height 1295 mm (51 in), wheelbase 2600 mm (102.4 in).

Unladen weight: 1693 kg (3731 lb).

Notes: Standard equipment includes air-conditioning, leather upholstery, front and rear head restraints, tinted glass and electric window lifts.

FERRARI (I)   Mondial 8

Identification: New Pininfarina-styled two-plus-two coupe to succeed Dino 308 and powered by similar mid and transverse-mounted 3-litre engine.

Engine: Centrally and transverse-mounted V-8-cylinder with four belt-driven overhead camshafts and Bosch K-Jetronic fuel injection. Bore × stroke 81 × 71 mm, displacement 2927 cc. Output 158 kW (215 bhp) @ 6600 rpm, torque 243 Nm (179 lb ft) @ 4600 rpm.

Transmission: Single-dry-plate clutch and five-speed manual gearbox. Rear-wheel drive.

Suspension: Front, independent with wishbones, coil springs, telescopic shock absorbers and anti-roll bar. Rear, independent with wishbones, coil springs, telescopic shock absorbers and anti-roll bar.

Steering: Rack and pinion.

Brakes: Ventilated discs front and rear, servo-assisted.

Tyres: 240/55 VR–390.

Dimensions: Length 4580 mm (180.3 in), width 1790 mm (70.5 in), height 1250 mm (49.2 in), wheelbase 2650 mm (104.3 in).

Unladen weight: 1445 kg (3185 lb).

Notes: Standard equipment includes air-conditioning, central door locking, digital instruments, speed control and electromagnetic opening of front and rear compartments and fuel-filler flap.

Identification: Larger-engined version of new economy car supplementing Panda 30 with basically similar specification but powered by twin-cylinder air-cooled 652 cc engine.

Engine: Front and transverse-mounted four-cylinder in-line with pushrod-operated overhead valves and Weber or Solex carburettor. Bore × stroke 65 × 68 mm, displacement 903 cc. Output 33 kW (45 bhp) @ 5600 rpm, torque 64 Nm (47 lb ft) @ 3000 rpm.

Transmission: Single-dry-plate clutch and four-speed manual gearbox. Front-wheel drive.

Suspension: Front, independent with MacPherson struts, coil springs, telescopic shock absorbers and anti-roll bar. Rear, dead axle with semi-elliptic springs and telescopic shock absorbers.

Steering: Rack and pinion.

Brakes: Discs front, drums rear, servo-assisted.

Tyres: 135 SR–13.

Dimensions: Length 3380 mm (133.1 in), width 1460 mm (57.5 in), height 1440 mm (56.7 in), wheelbase 2160 mm (85 in).

Unladen weight: 680 kg (1499 lb).

Notes: Standard equipment includes folding and removable rear seat, deep plastic front and rear bumpers and protective side mouldings.

Identification: Intermediate model in 127 range of three-door hatchback saloons bridging gap between L and Sport versions.

Engine: Front-mounted four-cylinder in-line with belt-driven overhead camshaft and Weber or Solex carburettor. Bore × stroke 76 × 57.8 mm, displacement 1049 cc. Output 37 kW (50 bhp) @ 5600 rpm, torque 77 Nm (57 lb ft) @ 3000 rpm.

Transmission: Single-dry-plate clutch and four-speed manual gearbox. Front-wheel drive.

Suspension: Front, independent with MacPherson struts, coil springs, telescopic shock absorbers and anti-roll bar. Rear, independent with MacPherson struts, transverse leaf spring and telescopic shock absorbers.

Steering: Rack and pinion.

Brakes: Discs front, drums rear, servo-assisted.

Tyres: 135 SR–13.

Dimensions: Length 3607 mm (142 in), width 1524 mm (60 in), height 1384 mm (54.5 in), wheelbase 2223 mm (87.5 in).

Unladen weight: 710 kg (1565 lb).

Notes: Standard equipment includes hinged rear side windows, rear screen wash/wipe, passenger door mirror and fabric upholstery.

FIAT (I)

128 1300

Identification: Remaining four-door saloon in rationalized 128 range, supplementing three-door estate car and bridging gap between 127 and Strada models.

Engine: Front and transverse-mounted four-cylinder in-line with belt-driven overhead camshaft and Weber carburettor. Bore × stroke 86.4 × 55.5 mm, displacement 1301 cc. Output 45 kW (60 bhp) @ 6000 rpm, torque 96 Nm (71 lb ft) @ 3200 rpm.

Transmission: Single-dry-plate clutch and four-speed manual gearbox. Front-wheel drive.

Suspension: Front, independent with MacPherson struts, coil springs, telescopic shock absorbers and anti-roll bar. Rear independent with MacPherson struts, transverse leaf spring and telescopic shock absorbers.

Steering: Rack and pinion.

Brakes: Discs front, drums rear, servo-assisted.

Tyres: 145 SR–13.

Dimensions: Length 3870 mm (152.4 in), width 1600 mm (63 in), height 1463 mm (57.6 in), wheelbase 2450 mm (96.5 in).

Unladen weight: 805 kg (1775 lb).

Notes: Standard equipment includes fabric upholstery, head restraints, reclining front seats and heated rear screen.

FIAT (I)

Strada 75 CL

Identification: Top model in range of three-door and five-door hatchbacks, known in Italy as Ritmo, supplementing 1.3-litre-engined 65 L and CL models.

Engine: Front and transverse-mounted four-cylinder in-line with belt-driven overhead camshaft and Weber carburettor. Bore × stroke 86.4 × 63.9 mm, displacement 1498 cc. Output 56 kW (75 bhp) @ 5800 rpm, torque 119 Nm (86 lb ft) @ 3000 rpm.

Transmission: Single-dry-plate clutch and five-speed manual gearbox, three-speed automatic transmission optional extra. Front-wheel drive.

Suspension: Front, independent with MacPherson struts, coil springs, telescopic shock absorbers and anti-roll bar. Rear, independent with MacPherson struts, transverse leaf spring, telescopic shock absorbers and anti-roll bar.

Steering: Rack and pinion.

Brakes: Discs front, drums rear, servo-assisted.

Tyres: 165/70 SR–13.

Dimensions: Length 3937mm (155 in), width 1650 mm (65 in), height 1400 mm (55.1 in), wheelbase 2450 mm (96.5in).

Unladen weight: 895 kg (1973 lb).

Notes: Standard equipment includes cloth upholstery, individually folding rear seats, two-speed wipers, laminated screen and tool kit.

FIAT (I)   Mirafiori 1600 CL

Identification: Intermediate model in Mirafiori range extending from 1.3-litre two-door and four-door saloons to 2-litre two-door Sport and 1.6-litre five-door estate cars.

Engine: Front-mounted four-cylinder in-line with pushrod-operated overhead valves and Weber or Solex carburettor. Bore × stroke 84 × 71.5 mm, displacement 1585 cc. Output 56 kW (75 bhp) @ 5400 rpm, torque 123 Nm (91 lb ft) @ 3000 rpm.

Transmission: Single-dry-plate clutch and five-speed manual gearbox, three-speed automatic transmission optional extra. Rear-wheel drive.

Suspension: Front, independent with MacPherson struts, coil springs, telescopic shock absorbers and anti-roll bar. Rear, live axle with trailing arms, Panhard rod, coil springs and telescopic shock absorbers.

Steering: Rack and pinion.

Brakes: Discs front, drums rear, servo-assisted.

Tyres: 165 SR–13.

Dimensions: Length 4260 mm (167.7 in), width 1650 mm (65 in), height 1390 mm (54.7 in), wheelbase 2490 mm (98 in).

Unladen weight: 1015 kg (2238 lb).

Notes: Standard equipment includes radio, fabric upholstery, head restraints, rev counter and clock.

FORD (GB & E)

Fiesta 1.3 GL

Identification: Addition to Fiesta range bridging gap between L and Ghia models and also available with 950 cc or 1.1-litre engine.

Engine: Front and transverse-mounted four-cylinder in-line with pushrod-operated overhead valves and Ford carburettor. Bore × stroke 81 × 63 mm, displacement 1298 cc. Output 49 kW (66 bhp) @ 5600 rpm, torque 94 Nm (68 lb ft) @ 3250 rpm.

Transmission: Single-dry-plate clutch and four-speed manual gearbox. Front-wheel drive.

Suspension: Front, independent with MacPherson struts, coil springs and telescopic shock absorbers. Rear, dead axle with trailing arms, coil springs and telescopic shock absorbers.

Steering: Rack and pinion.

Brakes: Discs front, drums rear, servo-assisted.

Tyres: 155 SR–12.

Dimensions: Length 3566 mm (140.4 in), width 1567 mm (61.7 in), height 1313 mm (51.7 in), wheelbase 2286 mm (90 in).

Unladen weight: 774 kg (1705 lb).

Notes: Standard equipment includes radio, load compartment carpet, halogen headlamps, body side mouldings and centre console.

FORD (GB & D)

Escort 1.1 L

Identification: Smallest-engined version of new Escort in five-door form and with L trim, supplementing base version and also offered as three-door saloon or estate car, and with 1.3 or 1.6-litre engine.

Engine: Front and transverse-mounted four-cylinder in-line with pushrod-operated overhead valves and Ford carburettor. Bore × stroke 74 × 65 mm, displacement 1116 cc. Output 41 kW (55 bhp) @ 5700 rpm, torque 83 Nm (61 lb ft) @ 4000 rpm.

Transmission: Single-dry-plate clutch and four-speed manual gearbox. Front-wheel drive.

Suspension: Front, independent with MacPherson struts, coil springs and telescopic shock absorbers. Rear, independent with coil springs, transverse arms, longitudinal tie-bars and telescopic shock absorbers.

Steering: Rack and pinion.

Brakes: Discs front, drums rear, servo-assisted.

Tyres: 145 SR–13 or 155 SR–13.

Dimensions: Length 3970 mm (156.3 in), width 1588 mm (62.5 in), height 1336 mm (52.6 in), wheelbase 2398 mm (94.4 in).

Unladen weight: 835 kg (1840 lb).

Notes: Standard equipment includes reclining front seats, three-speed heater fan, fabric upholstery, full door trim and tilting rear package tray.

FORD (GB & D)

Escort 1.3 Estate

Identification: Estate car version of new Escort, also available with 1.1-litre engine, and in L trim with 1.1, 1.3 or 1.6-litre engines.

Engine: Front and transverse-mounted four-cylinder in-line with belt-driven overhead camshaft and Ford carburettor. Bore × stroke 80 × 64.5 mm, displacement 1295 cc. Output 51 kW (69 bhp) @ 6000 rpm, torque 100 Nm (74 lb ft) @ 3500 rpm.

Transmission: Single-dry-plate clutch and four-speed manual gearbox. Front-wheel drive.

Suspension: Front, independent with MacPherson struts, coil springs, telescopic shock absorbers and anti-roll bar. Rear, independent with coil springs, transverse arms, longitudinal tie-bars and telescopic shock absorbers.

Steering: Rack and pinion.

Brakes: Discs front, drums rear, servo-assisted.

Tyres: 155 SR–13.

Dimensions: Length 3970 mm (156.3 in), width 1588 mm (62.5 in), height 1336 mm (52.6 in), wheelbase 2398 mm (94.4 in).

Unladen weight: 820 kg (1807 lb).

Notes: Standard equipment includes twin gas-filled tailgate support struts, 57.6 cubic feet of load space with rear seat folded and pushbutton tailgate release.

FORD (GB & D)

Escort 1.3 GL

Identification: Intermediate model in Escort saloon range, between L and Ghia versions, also available with three-door bodywork and 1.6-litre engine.

Engine: Front and transverse-mounted four-cylinder in-line with belt-driven overhead camshaft and Ford carburettor. Bore × stroke 80 × 64.5 mm, displacement 1295 cc. Output 51 kW (69 bhp) @ 6000 rpm, torque 100 Nm (74 lb ft) @ 3500 rpm.

Transmission: Single-dry-plate clutch and four-speed manual gearbox. Front-wheel drive.

Suspension: Front, independent with MacPherson struts, coil springs, telescopic shock absorbers and anti-roll bar. Rear, independent with coil springs, transverse arms, longitudinal tie-bars and telescopic shock absorbers.

Steering: Rack and pinion.

Brakes: Discs front, drums rear, servo-assisted.

Tyres: 175/70 SR–13.

Dimensions: Length 3970 mm (156.3 in), width 1588 mm (62.5 in), height 1336 mm (52.6 in), wheelbase 2398 mm (94.4 in).

Unladen weight: 855 kg (1884 lb).

Notes: Standard equipment includes halogen headlamps, push-button radio, analogue clock and carpeted load compartment with light.

FORD (GB & D)

Identification: Most luxuriously appointed model in new Escort range of three-door and five-door saloons, also available with 1.3-litre engine and three-door bodywork.

Engine: Front and transverse-mounted four-cylinder in-line with belt-driven overhead camshaft and Ford carburettor. Bore × stroke 80 × 79.5 mm, displacement 1596 cc. Output 59 kW (79 bhp) @ 5800 rpm, torque 125 Nm (92 lb ft) @ 3000 rpm.

Transmission: Single-dry-plate clutch and four-speed manual gearbox. Front-wheel drive.

Suspension: Front, independent with MacPherson struts, coil springs, telescopic shock absorbers and anti-roll bar. Rear, independent with coil springs, transverse arms, longitudinal tie-bars and telescopic shock absorbers.

Steering: Rack and pinion.

Brakes: Ventilated discs front, drums rear, servo-assisted.

Tyres: 155/80 SR–13.

Dimensions: Length 3970 mm (156.3 in), width 1588 mm (62.5 in), height 1336 mm (52.6 in), wheelbase 2398 mm (94.4 in).

Unladen weight: 890 kg (1962 lb).

Notes: Standard equipment includes velour-trimmed upholstery, head restraints, tilt/slide screened-glass sun roof and remote-control door mirrors.

FORD (D)   Escort XR3

Identification: High-performance model of new Escort range based on three-door bodyshell and incorporating uprated 1.6-litre engine, suspension and aerodynamic body changes.

Engine: Front and transverse-mounted four-cylinder in-line with belt-driven overhead camshaft and Weber twin-choke carburettor. Bore × stroke 80 × 79.5 mm, displacement 1596 cc. Output 72 kW (96 bhp) @ 6000 rpm, torque 133 Nm (98 lb ft) @ 4000 rpm.

Transmission: Single-dry-plate clutch and four-speed manual gearbox. Front-wheel drive.

Suspension: Front, independent with MacPherson struts, coil springs, gas-filled telescopic shock absorbers and anti-roll bar. Rear, independent with coil springs, transverse arms, longitudinal tie-bars and gas-filled telescopic shock absorbers.

Steering: Rack and pinion.

Brakes: Ventilated discs front, drums rear, servo-assisted.

Tyres: 185/60 HR–14.

Dimensions: Length 3970 mm (156.3 in), width 1588 mm (62.5 in), height 1336 mm (52.6 in), wheelbase 2398 mm (94.4 in).

Unladen weight: 895 kg (1973 lb).

Notes: Standard equipment includes front and rear spoilers, wheelarch air deflectors, tailgate wash/wipe, Recaro reclining seats and special interior trim.

FORD (GB)   Cortina 1600 L

Identification: Intermediate model in Britain's best-selling saloon range, bridging gap between base and GL models; also available with 1.3-litre engine and two-door bodywork and incorporating detail interior improvements.

Engine: Front-mounted four-cylinder in-line with belt-driven overhead camshaft and Ford carburettor. Bore × stroke 87.7 × 66 mm, displacement 1593 cc. Output 56 kW (75 bhp) @ 5500 rpm, torque 121 Nm (88 lb ft) @ 2800 rpm.

Transmission: Single-dry-plate clutch and four-speed manual gearbox, three-speed automatic transmission optional extra. Rear-wheel drive.

Suspension: Front, independent with wishbones, coil springs, telescopic shock absorbers and anti-roll bar. Rear, live axle with trailing arms, coil springs, telescopic shock absorbers and anti-roll bar.

Steering: Rack and pinion.

Brakes: Discs front, drums rear, servo-assisted.

Tyres: 165 SR–13.

Dimensions: Length 4340 mm (170.9 in), width 1700 mm (66.9 in), height 1360 mm (53.5 in), wheelbase 2578 mm (101.5 in).

Unladen weight: 1035 kg (2281 lb).

Notes: Standard equipment includes fabric upholstery, head restraints, laminated screen and front door bins.

FORD (GB)   Cortina 2300 Ghia Estate

Identification: Most luxurious model in Cortina estate-car range, supplementing standard, L. GL and GLS models with choice of 1.6, 2.0 and 2.3-litre engines.

Engine: Front-mounted V-6-cylinder with pushrod-operated overhead valves and Solex carburettor. Bore × stroke 90 × 60.1 mm, displacement 2294 cc. Output 87 kW (116 bhp) @ 5500 rpm, torque 182 Nm (132 lb ft) @ 3000 rpm.

Transmission: Single-dry-plate clutch and four-speed manual gearbox, three-speed automatic transmission optional extra. Rear-wheel drive.

Suspension: Front, independent with wishbones, coil springs, telescopic shock absorbers and anti-roll bar. Rear, live axle with trailing arms, coil springs, telescopic shock absorbers and anti-roll bar.

Steering: Rack and pinion, power assisted.

Brakes: Discs front, drums rear, servo-assisted.

Tyres: 185/70 SR–13.

Dimensions: Length 4480 mm (176.4 in), width 1700 mm (66.9 in), height 1367 mm (53.8in), wheelbase 2578 mm (101.5 in).

Unladen weight: 1197 kg (2639 lb).

Notes: Standard equipment includes alloy wheels, rev counter, velour upholstery and luxury carpeting.

Identification: Top sporting model in Capri range, supplement-ing more luxurious Ghia version and equipped with manual transmission and uprated detail equipment including new wider wheels.

Engine: Front-mounted V-6-cylinder with pushrod-operated overhead valves and Weber carburettor. Bore × stroke 93.7 × 72.4 mm, displacement 2994 cc. Output 101 kW (135 bhp) @ 5500 rpm, torque 238 Nm (172 lb ft) @ 3000 rpm.

Transmission: Single-dry-plate clutch and four-speed manual gearbox. Rear-wheel drive.

Suspension: Front, independent with MacPherson struts, coil springs, telescopic shock absorbers and anti-roll bar. Rear, live axle with semi-elliptic springs and telescopic shock absorbers.

Steering: Rack and pinion, power-assisted.

Brakes: Discs front, drums rear, servo-assisted.

Tyres: 185/70 HR–13.

Dimensions: Length 4374 mm (172.2 in), width 1700 mm (66.9 in), height 1288 mm (50.7 in), wheelbase 2563 mm (100.9 in).

Unladen weight: 1150 kg (2535 lb).

Notes: Standard equipment includes sports seats, head re-straints, front and rear spoilers, body side stripes and tinted glass.

FORD (D)   Granada 2.3 Ghia

Identification: Addition to Granada range combining Ghia coachwork and equipment with 2.3-litre V-6 engine also used for top Cortina Ghia.

Engine: Front-mounted V-6-cylinder with pushrod-operated overhead valves and Solex carburettor. Bore × stroke 90 × 60.1 mm, displacement 2294 cc. Output 84 kW (114 bhp) @ 5300 rpm, torque 181 Nm (129 lb ft) @ 3000 rpm.

Transmission: Single-dry-plate clutch and four-speed manual gearbox, three-speed automatic transmission optional extra. Rear-wheel drive.

Suspension: Front, independent with wishbones, coil springs, telescopic shock absorbers and anti-roll bar. Rear, independent with trailing arms, coil springs and telescopic shock absorbers.

Steering: Rack and pinion, power-assisted.

Brakes: Ventilated discs front, drums rear, servo-assisted.

Tyres: 190/65 HR–390.

Dimensions: Length 4653 mm (183.2 in), width 1793 mm (70.6 in), height 1379 mm (54.3 in), wheelbase 2769 mm (109 in).

Unladen weight: 1295 kg (2854 lb).

Notes: Standard equipment includes alloy wheels, tinted glass, electric window lifts, headlamp washers, central door locking and radio/stereo cassette player.

HONDA (J)   Civic 1300 3-door

Identification: Three-door version of larger-bodied Civic saloon, also offered in five-door form and powered by enlarged 1.3-litre engine.

Engine: Front and transverse-mounted four-cylinder in-line with belt-driven overhead camshaft and Keihin carburettor. Bore × stroke 72 × 82 mm, displacement 1335 cc. Output 44 kW (60 bhp) @ 5000 rpm, torque 97 Nm (69 lb ft) @ 3500 rpm.

Transmission: Single-dry-plate clutch and five-speed manual gearbox, two-speed semi-automatic transmission optional extra. Front-wheel drive.

Suspension: Front, independent with MacPherson struts, coil springs, telescopic shock absorbers and anti-roll bar. Rear, independent with MacPherson struts, coil springs and telescopic shock absorbers.

Steering: Rack and pinion.

Brakes: Discs front, drums rear, servo-assisted.

Tyres: 155 SR–13.

Dimensions: Length 3830 mm (150.8 in), width 1580 mm (62.2 in), height 1335 mm (52.6 in), wheelbase 2320 mm (91.3 in).

Unladen weight: 740 kg (1631 lb).

Notes: Standard equipment includes radio, three-speed heater fan, interior tailgate release, folding rear seat and tool kit.

HONDA (J)   Quintet

Identification: New five-door saloon supplementing three-door and five-door Accord and two-door Prelude models sharing same 1.6-litre engine.

Engine: Front and transverse-mounted four-cylinder in-line with belt-driven overhead camshaft and Keihin carburettor. Bore × stroke 77 × 86 mm, displacement 1602 cc. Output 59 kW (80 bhp) @ 5300 rpm, torque 130 Nm (93 lb ft) @ 3500 rpm.

Transmission: Single-dry-plate clutch and five-speed manual gearbox, three-speed semi-automatic transmission optional extra. Front-wheel drive.

Suspension: Front, independent with MacPherson struts, coil springs, telescopic shock absorbers and anti-roll bar. Rear, independent with MacPherson struts, coil springs, telescopic shock absorbers and anti-roll bar.

Steering: Rack and pinion, power-assistance optional extra.

Brakes: Discs front, drums rear, servo-assisted.

Tyres: 155 SR–13.

Dimensions: Length 4110 mm (161.8 in), width 1615 mm (63.6 in), height 1355 mm (53.4 in), wheelbase 2360 mm (92.9 in).

Unladen weight: 865 kg (1906 lb).

Notes: Standard equipment includes radio, cloth upholstery, tinted glass and rear screen wash/wipe.

JAGUAR (GB) XJ6 3.4

Identification: Subtly modified version of least expensive model in XJ6 range with detail improvements and slightly simplified specification.

Engine: Front-mounted six-cylinder in-line with twin chain-driven overhead camshafts and twin SU carburettors. Bore × stroke 83 × 106 mm, displacement 3442 cc. Output 120 kW (161 bhp) @ 5000 rpm, torque 261 Nm (189 lb ft) @ 3500 rpm.

Transmission: Single-dry-plate clutch and five-speed manual gearbox, three-speed automatic transmission optional extra. Rear-wheel drive.

Suspension: Front, independent with wishbones, coil springs, telescopic shock absorbers and anti-roll bar. Rear, independent with trailing arms, wishbones, fixed drive shafts, dual coil springs and telescopic shock absorbers.

Steering: Rack and pinion, power-assisted.

Brakes: Discs front and rear, servo-assisted.

Tyres: E70 VR–15.

Dimensions: Length 4959 mm (195.2 in), width 1770 mm (69.7 in), height 1377 mm (54 in), wheelbase 2866 mm (112.8 in).

Unladen weight: 1805 kg (3978 lb).

Notes: Standard equipment includes central door locking, radio, fabric upholstery, centre console and reversing lamps.

JAGUAR (GB) XJ6 4.2

Identification: Intermediate model in Series 3 Jaguar XJ range bridging gap between 3.4-litre carburettor-equipped model and 5.3-litre with fuel-injected V-12 engine as fitted to XJ-S coupe.

Engine: Front-mounted six-cylinder in-line with twin chain-driven overhead camshafts and Lucas-Bosch L-Jetronic electronic fuel injection. Bore × stroke 92 × 106 mm, displacement 4235 cc. Output 153 kW (205 bhp) @ 5000 rpm, torque 326 Nm (236 lb ft) @ 3750 rpm.

Transmission: Single-dry-plate clutch and five-speed manual gearbox or three-speed automatic transmission. Rear-wheel drive.

Suspension: Front, independent with wishbones, coil springs, telescopic shock absorbers and anti-roll bar. Rear, independent with trailing arms, wishbones, fixed drive shafts, dual coil springs and telescopic shock absorbers.

Steering: Rack and pinion, power-assisted.

Brakes: Discs front and rear, servo-assisted.

Tyres: E70 VR–15.

Dimensions: Length 4959 mm (195.2 in), width 1770 mm (69.7 in), height 1377 mm (54 in), wheelbase 2866 mm (112.8 in).

Unladen weight: 1830 kg (4033 lb).

Notes: Standard equipment includes stereo radio/cassette player, halogen headlamps, tinted glass and leather upholstery.

JAGUAR (GB) XJ-S

Identification: Two-plus-two-seater coupe with latest more powerful and more economical version of V-12 engine incorporating electronic digital fuel injection.

Engine: Front-mounted V-12-cylinder with single belt-driven overhead camshafts and Lucas-Bosch electronic digital fuel injection. Bore × stroke 90 × 70 mm, displacement 5343 cc. Output 224 kW (300 bhp) @ 5400 rpm, torque 423 Nm (318 lb ft) @ 3900 rpm.

Transmission: Three-speed automatic transmission. Rear-wheel drive.

Suspension: Front, independent with wishbones, coil springs, telescopic shock absorbers and anti-roll bar. Rear, independent with trailing arms, wishbones, fixed drive shafts, dual coil springs and telescopic shock absorbers.

Steering: Rack and pinion, power-assisted.

Brakes: Discs front and rear, servo-assisted.

Tyres: 205/70 VR–15.

Dimensions: Length 4869 mm (191.7 in), width 1793 mm (70.6 in), height 1262 mm (49.7 in), wheelbase 2591 mm (102 in).

Unladen weight: 1750 kg (3857 lb).

Notes: Standard equipment includes alloy wheels, air-conditioning, leather upholstery, tinted glass, electric window lifts and limited-slip differential.

LADA (R) 1600 ES

Identification: Revised version of most luxurious and powerful model in Lada range of four-door saloons and five-door estate cars incorporating new bumpers and lighting arrangements.

Engine: Front-mounted four-cylinder in-line with chain-driven overhead camshaft and Soviet carburettor. Bore × stroke 79 × 80 mm, displacement 1570 cc. Output 58 kW (78 bhp) @ 5400 rpm, torque 122 Nm (88 lb ft) @ 3000 rpm.

Transmission: Single-dry-plate clutch and four-speed manual gearbox. Rear-wheel drive.

Suspension: Front, independent with wishbones, coil springs, telescopic shock absorbers and anti-roll bar. Rear, live axle with trailing arms, Panhard rod, coil springs and telescopic shock absorbers.

Steering: Worm and roller.

Brakes: Discs front, drums rear, servo-assisted.

Tyres: 165 SR–13.

Dimensions: Length 4064 mm (160 in), width 1600 mm (63 in), height 1372 mm (54 in), wheelbase 2423 mm (95.4 in).

Unladen weight: 1030 kg (2270 lb).

Notes: Standard equipment includes vinyl roof covering, alloy wheels, heated rear screen and comprehensive tool kit.

LANCIA (I)   Delta 1500

Identification: Right-hand-drive version of top model in range of five-door saloons named as 1979 Car of the Year, also available with 1.3-litre engine.

Engine: Front and transverse-mounted four-cylinder in-line with belt-driven overhead camshaft and Weber carburettor. Bore × stroke 86.4 × 63.9 mm, displacement 1498 cc. Output 62.6 kW (85 bhp) @ 5800 rpm, torque 123 Nm (90.4 lb ft) @ 3500 rpm.

Transmission: Single-dry-plate clutch and five-speed manual gearbox. Front-wheel drive.

Suspension: Front, independent with MacPherson struts, coil springs, telescopic shock absorbers and anti-roll bar. Rear, independent with MacPherson struts, trailing and transverse links, coil springs and telescopic shock absorbers.

Steering: Rack and pinion.

Brakes: Discs front, drums rear, servo-assisted.

Tyres: 165/70 SR–13.

Dimensions: Length 3885 mm (153 in), width 1620 mm (63.8 in), height 1380 mm (54.3 in), wheelbase 2475 mm (97.4 in).

Unladen weight: 975 kg (2149 lb).

Notes: Standard equipment includes alloy wheels, split rear seat, velour upholstery and height-adjustable steering column.

LANCIA (I)   Montecarlo

Identification: Reintroduced coupe based on Beta design and incorporating front and rear styling changes and additional side windows for improved visibility.

Engine: Centrally and transverse-mounted four-cylinder in-line with twin belt-driven overhead camshafts and twin-choke Weber carburettor. Bore × stroke 84 × 90 mm, displacement 1995 cc. Output 89 kW (120 bhp) @ 6000 rpm, torque 171 Nm (126 lb ft) @ 3400 rpm.

Transmission: Single-dry-plate clutch and five-speed manual gearbox. Rear-wheel drive.

Suspension: Front, independent with MacPherson struts, coil springs, telescopic shock absorbers and anti-roll bar. Rear, independent with MacPherson struts, coil springs, telescopic shock absorbers and anti-roll bar.

Steering: Rack and pinion.

Brakes: Discs front and rear, servo-assisted.

Tyres: 185/65 HR–14.

Dimensions: Length 3815 mm (150.2 in), width 1695 mm (66.7 in), height 1190 mm (46.9 in), wheelbase 2300 mm (90.6 in).

Unladen weight: 1040 kg (2292 lb).

Notes: Standard equipment includes detachable roof section, head restraints, fabric upholstery and alloy wheels.

LANCIA (I)

Beta Trevi 2000

Identification: Intermediate model in three-car range of four-door saloons derived from Beta five-door hatchback saloons and bridging gap between 1.6-litre carburettor-equipped and 2-litre fuel-injected versions.

Engine: Front and transverse-mounted four-cylinder in-line with twin belt-driven overhead camshafts and twin-choke Weber carburettor. Bore × stroke 84 × 90 mm, displacement 1955 cc. Output 85 kW (115 bhp) @ 5500 rpm, torque 176 Nm (130 lb ft) @ 2800 rpm.

Transmission: Single-dry-plate clutch and five-speed manual gearbox, three-speed automatic transmission optional extra. Front-wheel drive.

Suspension: Front, independent with MacPherson struts, coil springs, telescopic shock absorbers and anti-roll bar. Rear, independent with MacPherson struts, coil springs, telescopic shock absorbers and anti-roll bar.

Steering: Rack and pinion, power-assisted.

Brakes: Discs front and rear, servo-assisted.

Tyres: 175/SR–14.

Dimensions: Length 4355 mm (171.4 in), width 1706 mm (67.1 in), height 1400 mm (55.1 in), wheelbase 2540 mm (100 in).

Unladen weight: 1165 kg (2568 lb).

Notes: Standard equipment includes fabric upholstery, front and rear head restraints, tinted glass and comprehensive instrumentation incorporating multiple warning-light system.

LAND-ROVER (GB)   V8 Station Wagon

Identification: UK-specification version of 3.5-litre-engined multi-purpose vehicle mounted on long-wheelbase chassis and supplementing four-cylinder short and long-wheelbase models.

Engine: Front-mounted V-8-cylinder with pushrod-operated overhead valves and twin Zenith-Stromberg carburettors. Bore × stroke 88.9 × 71.1 mm, displacement 3528 cc. Output 68 kW (91 bhp) @ 3500 rpm, torque 226 Nm (166 lb ft) @ 2000 rpm.

Transmission: Single-dry-plate clutch and four-speed manual gearbox with two-speed transfer box. Four-wheel drive.

Suspension: Front, rigid axle with semi-elliptic leaf springs and telescopic shock absorbers. Rear, rigid axle with semi-elliptic leaf springs and telescopic shock absorbers.

Steering: Recirculating ball.

Brakes: Drums front and rear, servo-assisted. Drum handbrake on rear of transfer box.

Tyres: 7.50 × 16.

Dimensions: Length 4445 mm (175 in), width 1690 mm (66.5 in), height 1920 mm (75.6 in), wheelbase 2768 mm (109 in).

Unladen weight: Approx. 1800 kg (3967 lb).

Notes: Standard equipment includes de luxe front seats, tinted glass, laminated screen, mudflaps, reversing lights and fresh-air heater.

Identification: Further improved version of four-wheel-drive all-purpose estate car incorporating interior changes including new seat facings, also available as five-door model by Monteverdi.

Engine: Front-mounted V-8-cylinder with pushrod-operated overhead valves and twin Zenith-Stromberg carburettors. Bore × stroke 88.9 × 71.1 mm, displacement 3528 cc. Output 97 kW (130 bhp) @ 5000 rpm, torque 256 Nm (185 lb ft) @ 2500 rpm.

Transmission: Single-dry-plate clutch and four-speed manual gearbox with two-speed transfer box. Four-wheel drive.

Suspension: Front, rigid axle with coil springs, radius arms, Panhard rod and telescopic shock absorbers. Rear, rigid axle with coil springs, radius arms, A-bracket and self-levelling struts.

Steering: Recirculating ball, power-assisted.

Brakes: Discs front and rear, servo-assisted. Drum brake on rear output shaft from transfer box.

Tyres: 205–16.

Dimensions: Length 4470 mm (176 in), width 1780 mm (70 in), height 1803 mm (71 in), wheelbase 2540 mm (100 in).

Unladen weight: 1725 kg (3802 lb).

Notes: Standard equipment includes head restraints, fabric upholstery, sliding rear side windows, tinted glass and mud flaps.

LOTUS (GB)

Eclat Series 2.2

Identification: Larger-engined derivative of Lotus four-seater two-door coupe incorporating aerodynamic body improvements and revised interior trim and equipment.

Engine: Front-mounted four-cylinder in-line with twin belt-driven overhead camshafts and twin Dellorto carburettors. Bore × stroke 95.3 × 76.2 mm, displacement 2174 cc. Output 120 kW (160 bhp) @ 6500 rpm, torque 224 Nm (160 lb ft) @ 5000 rpm.

Transmission: Single-dry-plate clutch and five-speed manual gearbox, three-speed automatic transmission optional extra. Rear-wheel drive.

Suspension: Front, independent with wishbones, coil springs, telescopic shock absorbers and anti-roll bar. Rear, independent with trailing arms, lateral links, coil springs and telescopic shock absorbers.

Steering: Rack and pinion, power-assistance optional extra.

Brakes: Discs front, drums rear, servo-assisted.

Tyres: 205/60 VR–14.

Dimensions: Length 4445 mm (175 in), width 1816 mm (71.5 in), height 1207 mm (47.5 in), wheelbase 2483 mm (97.8 in).

Unladen weight: 1102 kg (2429 lb).

Notes: Standard equipment includes alloy wheels, electric window lifts, rear screen wash/wipe, halogen headlamps, cloth trim and tinted glass.

Identification: Larger-engined derivative of Lotus four-seater hatchback coupe incorporating aerodynamic body improvements and revised interior trim and equipment.

Engine: Front-mounted four-cylinder in-line with twin belt-driven overhead camshafts and twin Dellorto carburettors. Bore × stroke 95.3 × 76.2 mm, displacement 2174 cc. Output 120 kW (160 bhp) @ 6500 rpm, torque 224 Nm (160 lb ft) @ 5000 rpm.

Transmission: Single-dry-plate clutch and five-speed manual gearbox, three-speed automatic transmission optional extra. Rear-wheel drive.

Suspension: Front, independent with wishbones, coil springs, telescopic shock absorbers and anti-roll bar. Rear, independent with trailing arms, lateral links, coil springs and telescopic shock absorbers.

Steering: Rack and pinion, power-assistance optional extra.

Brakes: Discs front, drums rear, servo-assisted.

Tyres: 205/60 VR–14.

Dimensions: Length 4445 mm (175 in), width 1816 mm (71.5 in), height 1207 mm (47.5 in), wheelbase 2483 mm (97.8 in).

Unladen weight: 1120 kg (2468 lb).

Notes: Standard equipment includes alloy wheels, electric window lifts, rear screen wash/wipe, halogen headlamps, cloth rim and tinted glass.

LOTUS (GB)   Esprit Series 2.2

Identification: Larger-engined derivative of Lotus two-seater mid-engined coupe incorporating new front spoiler and air intake and revised engine cover, alloy wheels, seats, instruments and rear lamps.

Engine: Mid-mounted four-cylinder in-line with twin belt-driven overhead camshafts and twin Dellorto carburettors. Bore × stroke 95.3 × 76.2 mm, displacement 2174 cc. Output 120 kW (160 bhp) @ 6500 rpm, torque 224 Nm (160 lb ft) @ 5000 rpm.

Transmission: Single-dry-plate clutch and five-speed manual gearbox. Rear-wheel drive.

Suspension: Front, independent with wishbones, coil springs, telescopic shock absorbers and anti-roll bar. Rear, independent with trailing arms, lateral links, coil springs and telescopic shock absorbers.

Steering: Rack and pinion.

Brakes: Discs front, drums rear, servo-assisted.

Tyres: 205/60 VR–14 front, 205/70 VR–14 rear.

Dimensions: Length 4191 mm (165 in), width 1854 mm (73 in), height 1111 mm (43.8 in), wheelbase 2438 mm (96 in).

Unladen weight: 1020 kg (2248 lb).

Notes: Standard equipment includes alloy wheels, electric window lifts, halogen headlamps, cloth trim, tinted glass and twin speakers.

Identification: Limited-edition derivative of Esprit S2 with turbocharged version of 2.2-litre engine, aerodynamic bodywork changes and improved cockpit layout.

Engine: Mid-mounted four-cylinder in-line with twin belt-driven overhead camshafts, exhaust-driven turbocharger and twin Dellorto carburettors. Bore × stroke 95.25 × 76.2 mm, displacement 2174 cc. Output 154 kW (210 bhp) @ 6000 rpm, torque 280 Nm (200 lb ft) @ 4500 rpm.

Transmission: Single-dry-plate clutch and five-speed manual gearbox. Rear-wheel drive.

Suspension: Front, independent with wishbones, coil springs, telescopic shock absorbers and anti-roll bar. Rear, independent with trailing arms, lateral links, coil springs and telescopic shock absorbers.

Steering: Rack and pinion.

Brakes: Discs front and rear, servo-assisted.

Tyres: 195/60 VR–15 front, 235/60 VR–15 rear.

Dimensions: Length 4191 mm (165 in), width 1854 mm (73 in), height 1118 in (44 in), wheelbase 2438 mm (96 in).

Unladen weight: 1220 kg (2690 lb).

Notes: Standard equipment includes oil cooler, air-conditioning, stereo radio/cassette player with four speakers, leather seats and trim and alloy wheels.

Identification: Latest version of Maserati mid-engined coupé featuring 3-litre engine, five-speed transmission and limited-slip differential with comprehensive interior equipment.

Engine: Centrally mounted V-6-cylinder with twin chain-driven overhead camshafts and triple Weber carburettors. Bore × stroke 91.6 × 75 mm, displacement 2965 cc. Output 155 kW (208 bhp) @ 5800 rpm, torque 255 Nm (188 lb ft) @ 5000 rpm.

Transmission: Single-dry-plate power-assisted clutch and five-speed manual gearbox. Rear-wheel drive.

Suspension: Front, independent with wishbones, coil springs, telescopic shock absorbers and anti-roll bar. Rear, independent with lower arms, coil springs, telescopic shock absorbers and anti-roll bar.

Steering: Rack and pinion, power-assisted.

Brakes: Ventilated discs front and rear, power-assisted.

Tyres: 195/70 VR–15.

Dimensions: Length 4318 mm (170 in), width 1768 mm (69.6 in), height 1133 mm (44.6 in), wheelbase 2598 mm (102.3 in).

Unladen weight: 1420 kg (3130 lb).

Notes: Standard equipment includes air-conditioning, electric window lifts, alloy wheels and tinted glass.

Identification: Smaller-engined version of Kyalami four-seater coupe, supplementing 4.9-litre offered with choice of manual gearbox or automatic transmission.

Engine: Front-mounted V-8-cylinder with twin chain-driven overhead camshafts and four Weber carburettors. Bore × stroke 86.3 × 83.8 mm, displacement 4136 cc. Output 190 kW (255 bhp) @ 6000 rpm, torque 393 Nm (290 lb ft) @ 3200 rpm.

Transmission: Single-dry-plate clutch and five-speed manual gearbox. Rear-wheel drive.

Suspension: Front, independent with wishbones, coil springs, telescopic shock absorbers and anti-roll bar. Rear, independent with trailing arms, transverse links, coil springs, telescopic shock absorbers and anti-roll bar.

Steering: Rack and pinion, power-assisted.

Brakes: Ventilated discs front and rear, servo-assisted.

Tyres: 205/70 VR–15.

Dimensions: Length 4572 mm (180 in), width 1849 mm (72.8 in), height 1270 mm (50 in), wheelbase 2598 mm (102.3 in).

Unladen weight: 1750 kg (3857 lb).

Notes: Standard equipment includes air-conditioning, electric window lifts, electronic ignition and tinted glass.

MAZDA (J)

323 1100 3-door

Identification: Lowest-priced and least powerful model in new range of front-wheel-drive cars embracing three- and five-door hatchbacks and in certain markets four-door saloons.

Engine: Front and transverse-mounted four-cylinder in-line with chain-driven overhead camshaft and Hitachi carburettor. Bore × stroke 70 × 69.6 mm, displacement 1071 cc. Output 41 kW (55 bhp) @ 6000 rpm, torque 79 Nm (58 lb ft) @ 4000 rpm.

Transmission: Single-dry-plate clutch and four-speed manual gearbox. Front-wheel drive.

Suspension: Front, independent with MacPherson struts, coil springs and telescopic shock absorbers. Rear, independent with MacPherson struts, coil springs, trailing and transverse links and anti-roll bar.

Steering: Rack and pinion.

Brakes: Discs front, drums rear, servo-assisted.

Tyres: 155 SR–13.

Dimensions: Length 3955 mm (155.7 in), width 1630 mm (64.1 in), height 1375 mm (54.1 in), wheelbase 2365 mm (93.1 in).

Unladen weight: 820 kg (1807 lb).

Notes: Standard equipment includes rear screen wash/wipe, reclining seats, quartz clock, halogen headlamps and tinted glass.

Identification: Intermediate model in five-door hatchback section of 323 range, bridging gap between 1.1 and 1.5-litre-engined versions.

Engine: Front and transverse-mounted four-cylinder in-line with chain-driven overhead camshaft and Hitachi dual-choke carburettor. Bore × stroke 77 × 69.6 mm, displacement 1296 cc. Output 51 kW (68 bhp) @ 6000 rpm, torque 96 Nm (70 lb ft) @ 3500 rpm.

Transmission: Single-dry-plate clutch and four-speed manual gearbox. Front-wheel drive.

Suspension: Front, independent with MacPherson struts, coil springs and telescopic shock absorbers. Rear, independent with MacPherson struts, coil springs, trailing and transverse links and anti-roll bar.

Steering: Rack and pinion.

Brakes: Discs front, drums rear, servo-assisted.

Tyres: 155 SR–13.

Dimensions: Length 3955 mm (155.7 in), width 1630 mm (64.2 in), height 1375 mm (54.1 in), wheelbase 2365 mm (93.1 in).

Unladen weight: 835 kg (1840 lb).

Notes: Standard equipment includes radio, three-speed heater fan, two-speed wipers with flick-wipe and intermittent facility, and electric engine-cooling fan.

MAZDA (J)

323 1500 GT

Identification: High-performance model in 323 range wit
three-door hatchback bodywork and higher level of mechanica
and equipment specification.

Engine: Front and transverse-mounted four-cylinder in-line wit
chain-driven overhead camshaft and twin Hitachi dual-chok
carburettors. Bore × stroke 77 × 80 mm, displacement 1490 c
Output 63 kW (85 bhp) @ 6000 rpm, torque 121 Nm (88 lb ft) (
3200 rpm.

Transmission: Single-dry-plate clutch and five-speed manua
gearbox. Front-wheel drive.

Suspension: Front, independent with MacPherson struts, co
springs, telescopic shock absorbers and anti-roll bar. Rea
independent with MacPherson struts, coil springs, trailing an
transverse arms and anti-roll bar.

Steering: Rack and pinion.

Brakes: Discs front, drums rear, servo-assisted.

Tyres: 175/70 SR-13.

Dimensions: Length 3955 m (155.7 in), width 1630 mm (64.
in), height 1375 mm (54.1 in), wheelbase 2365 mm (93.1 in).

Unladen weight: 850 kg (1873 lb).

Notes: Standard equipment includes alloy wheels, rear reclinin
seats, sun roof, rev counter, digital clock, sports steering whee
and adjustable steering rake.

MAZDA (J)　　　　　　　　　2000 Estate

Identification: Revised version of estate car introduced in 1979 and incorporating substantially changed front-end styling and additional side rubbing strips.

Engine: Front-mounted four-cylinder in-line with chain-driven overhead camshaft and Nikki carburettor. Bore × stroke 80 × 98 mm, displacement 1970 cc. Output 67 kW (90 bhp) @ 4800 rpm, torque 115 Nm (159 lb ft) @ 2500 rpm.

Transmission: Single-dry-plate clutch and four-speed manual gearbox, three-speed automatic transmission optional extra. Rear-wheel drive.

Suspension: Front, independent with MacPherson struts, coil springs, telescopic shock absorbers and anti-roll bar. Rear, live axle with semi-elliptic leaf springs and telescopic shock absorbers.

Steering: Recirculating ball.

Brakes: Discs front, drums rear, servo-assisted.

Tyres: 175 SR–14.

Dimensions: Length 4575 mm (180.1 in), width 1690 mm (66.5 in), height 1445 mm (56.9 in), wheelbase 2610 mm (102.8 in).

Unladen weight: 1190 kg (2623 lb).

Notes: Standard equipment includes halogen headlamps, tinted glass, rear screen wash/wipe, headlamp washers and electric tailgate operation.

Identification: Smallest petrol-engined model in W123 rang of four-door saloons, supplementing 2.3, 2.5 and 2.8-litre version and 2, 2.4 and 3-litre diesels.

Engine: Front-mounted four-cylinder in-line with chain-drive overhead camshaft and Bosch fuel injection. Bore × stroke 80 × 89 mm, displacement 1997 cc. Output 81 kW (109 bhp) 5200 rpm, torque 169 Nm (125 lb ft) @ 3000 rpm.

Transmission: Single-dry-plate clutch and four-speed manu gearbox. Rear-wheel drive.

Suspension: Front, independent with wishbones, coil spring telescopic shock absorbers and anti-roll bar. Rear, independe with trailing arms, swing axles, coil springs, telescopic shoc absorbers and anti-roll bar.

Steering: Recirculating ball, power-assisted.

Brakes: Discs front and rear, servo-assisted.

Tyres: 175 SR–14.

Dimensions: Length 4725 mm (186 in), width 1786 mm (70. in), height 1438 mm (56.6 in), wheelbase 2795 mm (110 in).

Unladen weight: 1330 kg (2931 lb).

Notes: Standard equipment includes internally adjustable rea view mirrors, built-in auxiliary lamps, head restraints and dir protected rear light clusters.

MERCEDES-BENZ (D) 230 CE

Identification: Replacement model for 230 C fitted with new and more powerful fuel-injected engine and supplementing 280 CE.

Engine: Front-mounted four-cylinder in-line with chain-driven overhead camshaft and Bosch fuel injection. Bore × stroke 80.3 × 95.5 mm, displacement 2299 cc. Output 101 kW (136 bhp) @ 5100 rpm, torque 205 Nm (151 lb ft) @ 3500 rpm.

Transmission: Four-speed automatic transmission or four-speed manual gearbox. Rear-wheel drive.

Suspension: Front, independent with wishbones, coil springs, telescopic shock absorbers and anti-roll bar. Rear, independent with trailing arms, swing axles, coil springs, telescopic shock absorbers and anti-roll bar.

Steering: Recirculating ball, power-assisted.

Brakes: Discs front and rear, servo-assisted.

Tyres: 195/70 HR–14.

Dimensions: Length 4640 mm (182.7 in), width 1786 mm (70.3 in), height 1395 mm (54.9 in), wheelbase 2710 mm (106.7 in).

Unladen weight: 1375 kg (3031 lb).

Notes: Standard equipment includes internally adjustable rear-view mirrors, head restraints and power-operated driver's seat lock.

Identification: Intermediate model in T-series range of five-door estate cars supplementing diesel-engined 240 TD and 300 TD and petrol-engined 280 TE versions.

Engine: Front-mounted six-cylinder in-line with chain-driven overhead camshaft and Solex carburettor. Bore × stroke 86 × 72.5 mm, displacement 2525 cc. Output 103 kW (140 bhp) @ 5500 rpm, torque 196 Nm (140 lb ft) @ 3500 rpm.

Transmission: Four-speed automatic transmission. Rear-wheel drive.

Suspension: Front, independent with wishbones, coil springs, telescopic shock absorbers and anti-roll bar. Rear, independent with semi-trailing arms, coil springs, self-levelling struts, telescopic shock absorbers and anti-roll bar.

Steering: Recirculating ball, power-assisted.

Brakes: Discs front and rear, servo-assisted.

Tyres: 195/70 HR–14.

Dimensions: Length 4724 mm (186 in), width 1784 mm (70.2 in), height 1425 mm (56.1 in), wheelbase 2794 mm (110 in).

Unladen weight: 1470 kg (3240 lb).

Notes: Standard equipment includes central door locking, split rear seat, twin roof rails, driver-adjustable headlamps and rear screen wash/wipe.

Identification: New smaller-engined version of SLC two-plus-two coupe, supplementing V-8-engined 380 SLC and featuring 2.8-litre engine also used in 280 E and 280 SE saloons, 280 CE coupe and 280 TE estate car.

Engine: Front-mounted six-cylinder in-line with twin overhead camshafts and Bosch fuel injection. Bore × stroke 86 × 78.8 mm, displacement 2746 cc. Output 136 kW (185 bhp) @ 5800 rpm, torque 240 Nm (174 lb ft) @ 4500 rpm.

Transmission: Four-speed automatic transmission. Rear-wheel drive.

Suspension: Front, independent with wishbones, coil springs, telescopic shock absorbers and anti-roll bar. Rear, independent with trailing arms, swing axles, coil springs, telescopic shock absorbers and anti-roll bar.

Steering: Recirculating ball, power-assisted.

Brakes: Discs front and rear, servo-assisted.

Tyres: 205/70 VR–14.

Dimensions: Length 4750 mm (187 in), width 1790 mm (70.5 in), height 1330 mm (52.4 in), wheelbase 2820 mm (111 in).

Unladen weight: 1550 kg (3416 lb).

Notes: Standard equipment includes head restraints, internally adjustable rear-view mirrors, rev counter, rear courtesy light and fabric upholstery.

Identification: Highest-specification model in range of SL two-seaters, supplementing V-8-powered 380 SL and six-cylinder-engined 280 SL.

Engine: Front-mounted V-8-cylinder with chain-driven overhead camshafts and Bosch mechanical fuel injection. Bore × stroke 96.5 × 85 mm, displacement 4973 cc. Output 177 kW (240 bhp) @ 4750 rpm, torque 404 Nm (292 lb ft) @ 3200 rpm

Transmission: Four-speed automatic transmission. Rear-wheel drive.

Suspension: Front, independent with wishbones, coil springs telescopic shock absorbers and anti-roll bar. Rear, independent with trailing arms, swing axles, coil springs, telescopic shock absorbers and anti-roll bar.

Steering: Recirculating ball, power-assisted.

Brakes: Discs front and rear, servo-assisted.

Tyres: 205/70 VR–14.

Dimensions: Length 4390 mm (172.8 in), width 1790 mm (70.5 in), height 1300 mm (51.2 in), wheelbase 2460 mm (96.9 in).

Unladen weight: Approx. 1515 kg (3339 lb).

Notes: Standard equipment includes head restraints, internally adjustable rear-view mirrors, rev counter and front and rear spoilers.

MERCEDES-BENZ (D)

380 SE

Identification: Intermediate model in new S-series range, bridging gap between 280 SE and 500 SE and also available on longer-wheelbase chassis as 380 SEL.

Engine: Front-mounted V-8-cylinder with chain-driven overhead camshafts and Bosch mechanical fuel injection. Bore × stroke 92 × 71.8 mm, displacement 3818 cc. Output 160 kW (218 bhp) @ 5500 rpm, torque 305 Nm (221 lb ft) @ 4000 rpm.

Transmission: Four-speed automatic transmission. Rear-wheel drive.

Suspension: Front, independent with wishbones, coil springs, telescopic shock absorbers and anti-roll bar. Rear, independent with trailing arms, swing axles, coil springs, telescopic shock absorbers and anti-roll bar.

Steering: Recirculating ball, power-assisted.

Brakes: Discs front and rear, servo-assisted.

Tyres: 205/70 VR–14.

Dimensions: Length 4995 mm (196.7 in), width 1820 mm (71.7 in), height 1436 mm (56.6 in), wheelbase 2935 mm (115.6 in).

Unladen weight: 1595 kg (3515 lb).

Notes: Standard equipment includes height-adjustable front seat belts, three rear seat belts, deformable bumpers, central locking, electric window lifts, headlamp wash/wipe and tinted glass.

MERCEDES-BENZ (D) 500 SEL

Identification: Top model in new S-series range, supplementing 380 SEL and standard-wheelbase 280 SE, 380 SE and 500 SE models.

Engine: Front-mounted V-8-cylinder with chain-driven overhead camshafts and Bosch mechanical fuel injection. Bore × stroke 96.5 × 85 mm, displacement 4973 cc. Output 177 kW (240 bhp) @ 4750 rpm, torque 404 Nm (292 lb ft) @ 3200 rpm.

Transmission: Four-speed automatic transmission. Rear-wheel drive.

Suspension: Front, independent with wishbones, coil springs, telescopic shock absorbers and anti-roll bar. Rear, independent with trailing arms, swing axles, coil springs, telescopic shock absorbers and anti-roll bar.

Steering: Recirculating ball, power-assisted.

Brakes: Discs front and rear, servo-assisted.

Tyres: 205/70 VR–14.

Dimensions: Length 5135 mm (202.2 in), width 1820 mm (71.7 in), height 1440 mm (56.7 in), wheelbase 3075 mm (121.1 in).

Unladen weight: 1655 kg (3648 lb).

Notes: Standard equipment includes air-conditioning, anti-lock braking, cruise control, limited-slip differential, central locking, electric window lifts, four head restraints, headlamp wash/wipe and tinted glass.

Identification: Senior model in realigned Mini range supplementing Mini City and powered by 1-litre A-series engine.

Engine: Front and transverse-mounted four-cylinder in-line with pushrod-operated overhead valves and SU carburettor. Bore × stroke 64.6 × 76.2 mm, displacement 998 cc. Output 29 kW (39 bhp) @ 4750 rpm, torque 69 Nm (51 lb ft) @ 2000 rpm.

Transmission: Single-dry-plate clutch and four-speed manual gearbox. Front-wheel drive.

Suspension: Front, independent with wishbones, rubber cone springs and telescopic shock absorbers. Rear, independent with trailing arms, rubber cone springs and telescopic shock absorbers.

Steering: Rack and pinion.

Brakes: Drums front and rear.

Tyres: 145 SR–10.

Dimensions: Length 3056 mm (120.3 in), width 1410 mm (55.5 in), height 1346 mm (53 in), wheelbase 2037 mm (80.2 in).

Unladen weight: 615 kg (1355 lb).

Notes: Standard equipment includes fabric upholstery, face-level air vents, reclining front seats and opening rear side windows.

MORRIS (GB)   Ital 1.3 HL

Identification: Intermediate model of 1.3-litre version four-door saloons and five-door estate cars supplementing L and HLS models and based on Morris Marina with bodywork restyled by Ital Design.

Engine: Front-mounted four-cylinder in-line with pushrod-operated overhead valves and SU carburettor. Bore × stroke 70.6 × 81.3 mm, displacement 1275 cc. Output 45 kW (61 bhp) @ 5300 rpm, torque 97 Nm (69 lb ft) @ 2950 rpm.

Transmission: Single-dry-plate clutch and four-speed manual gearbox, three-speed automatic transmission optional extra. Rear-wheel drive.

Suspension: Front, independent with wishbones, torsion bars, lever-type shock absorbers and anti-roll bar. Rear, live axle with semi-elliptic springs, telescopic shock absorbers and anti-roll bar.

Steering: Rack and pinion.

Brakes: Discs front, drums rear, servo-assisted.

Tyres: 155 SR–13.

Dimensions: Length 4343 mm (171 in), width 1636 mm (64.4 in), height 1418 mm (55.8 in), wheelbase 2438 mm (96 in).

Unladen weight: 939 kg (2070 lb).

Notes: Standard equipment includes radio, rear mudflaps, halogen headlamps, reclining front seats and luggage compartment lamp.

MORRIS (GB)

Ital 1.7L Estate

Identification: Least expensive 1.7-litre-engined Ital estate car, supplementing HL and HLS models. L estate also available with 1.3-litre engine.

Engine: Front-mounted four-cylinder in-line with belt-driven overhead camshaft and SU carburettor. Bore × stroke 84.5 × 75.8 mm, displacement 1698 cc. Output 58 kW (78 bhp) @ 5150 rpm, torque 129 Nm (93 lb ft) @ 3400 rpm.

Transmission: Single-dry-plate clutch and four-speed manual gearbox. Rear-wheel drive.

Suspension: Front, independent with wishbones, torsion bars, lever-type shock absorbers and anti-roll bar. Rear, live axle with semi-elliptic springs and telescopic shock absorbers.

Steering: Rack and pinion.

Brakes: Discs front, drums rear, servo-assisted.

Tyres: 155 SR–13.

Dimensions: Length 4378 mm (172.2 in), width 1636 mm (64.4 in), height 1418 mm (55.8in), wheelbase 2438 mm (96 in).

Unladen weight: 970 kg (2139 lb).

Notes: Standard equipment includes reversing lamp, electric screen washers, illuminated load compartment and heated rear screen.

MORRIS (GB)

Ital 2000 HLS

Identification: Top model in Ital range of saloons and estate cars supplementing L and HL versions with 1.3-litre A-series or 1.7-litre O-series engine.

Engine: Front-mounted four-cylinder in-line with belt-driven overhead camshaft and SU carburettor. Bore × stroke 84.5 × 89 mm, displacement 1993 cc. Output 70 kW (93 bhp) @ 4900 rpm, torque 156 Nm (113 lb ft) @ 3400 rpm.

Transmission: Three-speed automatic transmission. Rear-wheel drive.

Suspension: Front, independent with wishbones, torsion bars, lever-type shock absorbers and anti-roll bar. Rear, live axle with semi-elliptic springs, telescopic shock absorbers and anti-roll bar.

Steering: Rack and pinion.

Brakes: Discs front, drums rear, servo-assisted.

Tyres: 165 SR–13.

Dimensions: Length 4343 mm (171 in), width 1636 mm (64.4 in), height 1418 mm (55.8 in), wheelbase 2438 mm (96 in).

Unladen weight: Approx. 1000 kg (2204 lb).

Notes: Standard equipment includes vinyl roof, tinted glass, head restraints, fabric upholstery and front spoiler.

OLDSMOBILE (USA)

Delta 88 Royale Brougham

Identification: Top model in six-car Delta 88 series of saloons and coupes bridging gap between Cutlass and Delta 98 ranges.

Engine: Front-mounted V-6-cylinder with pushrod-operated overhead valves and Rochester carburettor. Bore × stroke 96.5 × 86.4 mm, displacement 3785 cc. Output 81 kW (110 bhp) @ 3800 rpm, torque 256 Nm (190 lb ft) @ 1600 rpm.

Transmission: Three-speed automatic transmission. Rear-wheel drive.

Suspension: Front, independent with wishbones, coil springs, telescopic shock absorbers and anti-roll bar. Rear, live axle with trailing arms, lateral links, coil springs and telescopic shock absorbers.

Steering: Recirculating ball, power-assisted.

Brakes: Discs front, drums rear, servo-assisted.

Tyres: 205/75 HR–15.

Dimensions: Length 5540 mm (218.1 in), width 1938 mm (76.3 in), height 1422 mm (56 in), wheelbase 2946 mm (116 in).

Unladen weight: 1640 kg (3615 lb).

Notes: Standard equipment includes dual headlamps, head restraints, transistorized ignition and individual front seats.

OPEL (D)   Kadett 1.3 Hatch 5-door

Identification: Intermediate model in revised Kadett range embracing two-door and four-door saloons, three-door and five-door hatchbacks and three-door and five-door estate cars with 1.2-litre or 1.3-litre engine.

Engine: Front and transverse-mounted four-cylinder in-line with belt-driven overhead camshaft and Solex carburettor. Bore × stroke 75 × 73.4 mm, displacement 1297 cc. Output 45 kW (60 bhp) @ 5800 rpm, torque 94 Nm (69 lb ft) @ 3400 rpm.

Transmission: Single-dry-plate clutch and four-speed manual gearbox. Front-wheel drive.

Suspension: Front, independent with MacPherson struts, coil springs, telescopic shock absorbers and anti-roll bar. Rear, dead axle with trailing arms, coil springs, telescopic shock absorbers and anti-roll bar.

Steering: Rack and pinion.

Brakes: Discs front, drums rear, servo-assisted.

Tyres: 155 SR–13.

Dimensions: Length 4000 mm (157.5 in), width 1640 mm (64.6 in), height 1380 mm (54.3 in), wheelbase 2515 mm (99 in).

Unladen weight: 855 kg (1885 lb).

Notes: Standard equipment includes rear screen wash/wipe, clock, fabric upholstery and head restraints.

Identification: High-performance derivative of Ascona two-door saloon with enlarged engine incorporating twin-overhead-camshafts and uprated transmission and suspension plus aerodynamic body changes.

Engine: Front-mounted four-cylinder in-line with twin chain-driven overhead camshafts and Bosch fuel injection. Bore × stroke 95 × 85 mm, displacement 2410 cc. Output 107 kW (144 bhp) @ 5200 rpm, torque 210 Nm (155 lb ft) @ 3800 rpm.

Transmission: Single-dry-plate clutch and five-speed manual gearbox. Rear-wheel drive.

Suspension: Front, independent with wishbones, coil springs, telescopic shock absorbers and anti-roll bar. Rear, live axle with trailing and lateral arms, coil springs, telescopic shock absorbers and anti-roll bar.

Steering: Rack and pinion.

Brakes: Discs front, drums rear, servo-assisted.

Tyres: 205/50 VR-15.

Dimensions: Length 4320 mm (170.1 in), width 1664 mm (65.5 in), height 1372 mm (54 in), wheelbase 2518 mm (99.1 in).

Unladen weight: 1050 kg (2314 lb).

Notes: Standard equipment includes limited-slip differential, alloy wheels, headlamp wash/wipe, front and rear spoilers, body side extensions and wing fins and competition-type seats with fabric trim.

OPEL (D)

Manta GT/J

Identification: Sporting derivative of Manta Berlinetta incorporating exterior styling features including body stripes and uprated suspension and steering.

Engine: Front-mounted four-cylinder in-line with chain-driven overhead camshaft and GM carburettor. Bore × stroke 95 × 69.8 mm, displacement 1979 cc. Output 74 kW (100 bhp) @ 5400 rpm, torque 148 Nm (107 lb ft) @ 3800 rpm.

Transmission: Single-dry-plate clutch and four-speed manual gearbox. Rear-wheel drive.

Suspension: Front, independent with wishbones, coil springs, telescopic shock absorbers and anti-roll bar. Rear, live axle with trailing arms, lateral links, coil springs, telescopic shock absorbers and anti-roll bar.

Steering: Rack and pinion.

Brakes: Discs front, drums rear, servo-assisted.

Tyres: 185/70 HR–13.

Dimensions: Length 4445 mm (175 in), width 1676 mm (66 in), height 1321 mm (52 in), wheelbase 2515 mm (99 in).

Unladen weight: Approx. 1000 kg (2204 lb).

Notes: Standard equipment includes full instrumentation, laminated screen, remote-control rear-view mirror and halogen headlamps.

OPEL (D)   Commodore Berlina CD

Identification: Top-specification version of intermediate four-door saloon bridging gap between Rekord and Senator models and based on modified Rekord bodyshell.

Engine: Front-mounted six-cylinder in-line with chain-driven overhead camshaft and Zenith carburettor. Bore × stroke 87 × 69.8 mm, displacement 2490 cc. Output 85 kW (115 bhp) @ 5200 rpm, torque 179 Nm (132 lb ft) @ 3800 rpm.

Transmission: Single-dry-plate clutch and four-speed manual gearbox, four-speed-and-overdrive gearbox or three-speed automatic transmission optional extra. Rear-wheel drive.

Suspension: Front, independent with MacPherson struts, coil springs, telescopic shock absorbers and anti-roll bar. Rear, live axle with four-link system, coil springs, telescopic shock absorbers and anti-roll bar.

Steering: Recirculating ball, power-assisted.

Brakes: Discs front, drums rear, servo-assisted.

Tyres: 195/70 HR–14.

Dimensions: Length 4732 mm (186.3 in), width 1722 mm (67.8 in), height 1410 mm (55.5 in), wheelbase 2667 mm (105 in).

Unladen weight: 1220 kg (2690 lb).

Notes: Standard equipment includes sliding sun roof, alloy wheels, central door locking, electric window lifts, front and rear head restraints and velour upholstery.

Identification: Larger-engined derivative of Senator 2.8S saloon with 3-litre instead of 2.8-litre engine and supplementing 3.0 CD fuel-injected model.

Engine: Front-mounted six-cylinder in-line with chain-driven overhead camshaft and Solex carburettor. Bore × stroke 95 × 69.8 mm, displacement 2968 cc. Output 110 kW (150 bhp) @ 5200 rpm, torque 230 Nm (170 lb ft) @ 3400 rpm.

Transmission: Single-dry-plate clutch and four-speed manual gearbox, three-speed automatic transmission optional extra. Rear-wheel drive.

Suspension: Front, independent with MacPherson struts, coil springs, telescopic shock absorbers and anti-roll bar. Rear, independent with trailing arms, coil springs, telescopic shock absorbers and anti-roll bar.

Steering: Recirculating ball, power-assisted.

Brakes: Ventilated discs front, discs rear, servo-assisted.

Tyres: 195/70 HR–14.

Dimensions: Length 4877 mm (192 in), width 1726 mm (68 in), height 1366 mm (53.8 in), wheelbase 2683 mm (105.6 in).

Unladen weight: 1375 kg (3031 lb).

Notes: Standard equipment includes central locking, fabric upholstery, head restraints, alloy wheels and tinted glass.

Identification: Smallest-engined version of revised 104 range of three-door and five-door saloons incorporating improved exterior styling and interior specification.

Engine: Front and transverse-mounted four-cylinder in-line with chain-driven overhead camshaft and Solex carburettor. Bore × stroke 70 × 62 mm, displacement 954 cc. Output 33 kW (45 bhp) @ 6000 rpm, torque 66 Nm (47 lb ft) @ 3000 rpm.

Transmission: Single-dry-plate clutch and four-speed manual gearbox. Front-wheel drive.

Suspension: Front, independent with MacPherson struts, coil springs, telescopic shock absorbers and anti-roll bar. Rear, independent with trailing arms, coil springs, telescopic shock absorbers and anti-roll bar.

Steering: Rack and pinion.

Brakes: Discs front, drums rear.

Tyres: 135 SR–13.

Dimensions: Length 3366 mm (132.5 in), width 1520 mm (59.8 in), height 1340 mm (52.8 in), wheelbase 2230 mm (87.8 in).

Unladen weight: 780 kg (1719 lb).

Notes: Standard equipment includes adjustable headlamps, heated rear screen, cloth upholstery and rear parcels shelf.

Identification: High-performance model in 104 range combining 1.3-litre engine with three-door bodywork and uprated suspension.

Engine: Front and transverse-mounted four-cylinder in-line with chain-driven overhead camshaft and Solex carburettor. Bore × stroke 75 × 77 mm, displacement 1360 cc. Output 54 kW (72 bhp) @ 6000 rpm, torque 109 Nm (79 lb ft) @ 3000 rpm.

Transmission: Single-dry-plate clutch and four-speed manual gearbox. Front-wheel drive.

Suspension: Front, independent with MacPherson struts, coil springs, telescopic shock absorbers and anti-roll bar. Rear, independent with trailing arms, coil springs, telescopic shock absorbers and anti-roll bar.

Steering: Rack and pinion.

Brakes: Discs front, drums rear, servo-assisted.

Tyres: 165/70 SR–13.

Dimensions: Length 3366 mm (132.5 in), width 1520 mm (59.8 in), height 1340 mm (52.8 in), wheelbase 2230 mm (87.8 in).

Unladen weight: 800 kg (1763 lb).

Notes: Standard equipment includes electric window lifts, rev counter, tinted glass, halogen headlamps and laminated screen.

PEUGEOT (F)   104 SR

Identification: Intermediate model in 104 range of five-door saloons with new 1.2-litre engine bridging gap between 1.1-litre GR and 1.3-litre S models.

Engine: Front and transverse-mounted four-cylinder in-line with chain-driven overhead camshaft and Solex carburettor. Bore × stroke 75 × 69 mm, displacement 1219 cc. Output 42 kW (57 bhp) @ 5500 rpm, torque 95 Nm (68 lb ft) @ 2750 rpm.

Transmission: Single-dry-plate clutch and four-speed manual gearbox. Front-wheel drive.

Suspension: Front, independent with MacPherson struts, coil springs, telescopic shock absorbers and anti-roll bar. Rear, independent with trailing arms, coil springs, telescopic shock absorbers and anti-roll bar.

Steering: Rack and pinion.

Brakes: Discs front, drums rear.

Tyres: 145 SR–13.

Dimensions: Length 3620 mm (142.5 in), width 1520 mm (59.8 in), height 1340 mm (52.8 in), wheelbase 2420 mm (95.3 in).

Unladen weight: 800 kg (1763 lb).

Notes: Standard equipment includes reclining front seats, tweed cloth upholstery, head restraints and side protective body mouldings.

PEUGEOT (F)

305 GLS

Identification: Additional model to 305 range combining specification of 305 GL with 1.5-litre engine of 305 SR saloon.

Engine: Front and transverse-mounted four-cylinder in-line with chain-driven overhead camshaft and Solex carburettor. Bore × stroke 78 × 77 mm, displacement 1472 cc. Output 55 kW (74 bhp) @ 5700 rpm, torque 118 Nm (85 lb ft) @ 3000 rpm.

Transmission: Single-dry-plate clutch and four-speed manual gearbox. Front-wheel drive.

Suspension: Front, independent with MacPherson struts, coil springs, telescopic shock absorbers and anti-roll bar. Rear, independent with semi-trailing arms, coil springs, telescopic shock absorbers and anti-roll bar.

Steering: Rack and pinion.

Brakes: Discs front, drums rear, servo-assisted.

Tyres: 145 SR–14.

Dimensions: Length 4237 mm (166.8 in), width 1613 mm (63.5 in), height 1405 mm (55.3 in), wheelbase 2624 mm (103.3 in).

Unladen weight: 940 kg (2072 lb).

Notes: Standard equipment includes reclining front seats, cloth and vinyl upholstery, rear fog lamps and reversing lamps.

PEUGEOT (F)

305 SR Estate

Identification: Five-door estate car derivative of 305 four-door saloons with rear suspension modifications to provide maximum rear load area.

Engine: Front and transverse-mounted four-cylinder in-line with chain-driven overhead camshaft and Solex carburettor. Bore × stroke 78 × 77 mm, displacement 1472 cc. Output 55 kW (74 bhp) @ 5700 rpm, torque 118 Nm (85 lb ft) @ 3000 rpm.

Transmission: Single-dry-plate clutch and four-speed manual gearbox. Front-wheel drive.

Suspension: Front, independent with MacPherson struts, coil springs, telescopic shock absorbers and anti-roll bar. Rear, independent with trailing arms, coil springs, telescopic shock absorbers and anti-roll bar.

Steering: Rack and pinion.

Brakes: Discs front, drums rear, servo-assisted.

Tyres: 145 SR–14.

Dimensions: Length 4237 mm (166.8 in), width 1630 mm (64.2 in), height 1405 mm (55.3 in), wheelbase 2624 mm (103.3 in).

Unladen weight: 965 kg (2127 lb).

Notes: Standard equipment includes reclining seats, head restraints, rear screen wash/wipe and fabric upholstery.

PEUGEOT (F) 505 SR

Identification: Intermediate model in range of four-door saloons with higher specification level than 505 GR and similar to that of fuel-injected 505 STI and diesel-engined 505 SRD versions.

Engine: Front-mounted four-cylinder in-line with chain-driven overhead camshaft and Zenith carburettor. Bore × stroke 88 × 81 mm, displacement 1971 cc. Output 69 kW (96 bhp) @ 5200 rpm, torque 160 Nm (118 lb ft) @ 3000 rpm.

Transmission: Single-dry-plate clutch and four-speed manual gearbox, three-speed automatic transmission optional extra. Rear-wheel drive.

Suspension: Front, independent with MacPherson struts, coil springs, telescopic shock absorbers and anti-roll bar. Rear, independent with trailing arms, coil springs, telescopic shock absorbers and anti-roll bar.

Steering: Rack and pinion, power-assisted.

Brakes: Discs front, drums rear, servo-assisted.

Tyres: 175 HR–14.

Dimensions: Length 4580 mm (180.3 in), width 1720 mm (67.7 in), height 1450 mm (57.1 in), wheelbase 2740 mm (107.9 in).

Unladen weight: 1200 kg (2645 lb).

Notes: Standard equipment includes velour upholstery, tinted glass, laminated screen, electric window lifts and sliding roof.

Identification: Turbocharged diesel-engined addition to top range of four-door saloons with high-level specification and manual transmission.

Engine: Front-mounted four-cylinder in-line with pushrod-operated overhead valves, exhaust-driven turbocharger and Bosch diesel fuel injection. Bore × stroke 94 × 83 mm, displacement 2304 cc. Output 59 kW (80 bhp) @ 4150 rpm, torque 190 Nm (136 lb ft) @ 2000 rpm.

Transmission: Single-dry-plate clutch and five-speed manual gearbox. Rear-wheel drive.

Suspension: Front, independent with MacPherson struts, coil springs, telescopic shock absorbers and anti-roll bar. Rear, independent with trailing arms, coil springs, telescopic shock absorbers and anti-roll bar.

Steering: Rack and pinion, power-assisted.

Brakes: Discs front and rear, servo-assisted.

Tyres: 175 HR–14.

Dimensions: Length 4721 mm (185.8 in), width 1770 mm (69.7 in), height 1457 mm (57.4 in), wheelbase 2800 mm (110.2 in).

Unladen weight: 1465 kg (3229 lb).

Notes: Standard equipment includes velour upholstery, electric window lifts and sliding roof and central door, window and roof locking.

PONTIAC (USA)　　　Grand Prix Brougham

Identification: New top model in three-car range of two-door notchback coupes, supplementing standard and LJ versions and incorporating luxury interior specification.

Engine: Front-mounted V-6-cylinder with pushrod-operated overhead valves and Rochester carburettor. Bore × stroke 96.5 × 86.4 mm, displacement 3785 cc. Output 85 kW (115 bhp) @ 3000 rpm, torque 256 Nm (190 lb ft) @ 2000 rpm.

Transmission: Three-speed automatic transmission. Rear wheel drive.

Suspension: Front, independent with wishbones, coil springs, telescopic shock absorbers and anti-roll bar. Rear, live axle with trailing arms, lateral links, coil springs and telescopic shock absorbers.

Steering: Recirculating ball, power-assisted.

Brakes: Discs front, drums rear, servo-assisted.

Tyres: 195/75 HR–14.

Dimensions: Length 5116 mm (201.4 in), width 1847 mm (72.7 in), height 1354 mm (53.3 in), wheelbase 2746 mm (108.1 in).

Unladen weight: Approx. 1500 kg (3306 lb).

Notes: Standard equipment includes velour upholstery, electric window lifts, vinyl roof, wood-grained door trim and interior opera lamps.

PORSCHE (D) 924 Turbo

Identification: Higher-powered and more economical version of previous 924 Turbo, also incorporating minor detail changes including side repeater lights.

Engine: Front-mounted four-cylinder in-line with KKK exhaust-driven turbocharger, belt-driven overhead camshaft and Bosch K-Jetronic fuel injection. Bore × stroke 86.5 × 84.4 mm, displacement 1984 cc. Output 132 kW (177 bhp) @ 5500 rpm, torque 251 Nm (185 lb ft) @ 3500 rpm.

Transmission: Single-dry-plate clutch and rear-mounted five-speed manual gearbox. Rear-wheel drive.

Suspension: Front, independent with MacPherson struts, coil springs, telescopic shock absorbers and anti-roll bar. Rear, independent with trailing arms, torsion bars, telescopic shock absorbers and anti-roll bar.

Steering: Rack and pinion.

Brakes: Ventilated discs front and rear, servo-assisted.

Tyres: 185/70 VR–15 or 205/55 VR–16.

Dimensions: Length 4212 mm (165.8 in), width 1685 mm (66.3 in), height 1270mm (50in), wheelbase 2400 mm (94.5 in).

Unladen weight: 1180 kg (2601 lb).

Notes: Standard equipment includes electrically operated windows, side repeater flashers on front wings and digital ignition system.

PORSCHE (D)

924 Carrera GT

Identification: Production version of prototype competition-orientated derivative of Porsche 924 built in 1979 with bodywork modifications, wider wheels and uprated engine and running gear.

Engine: Front-mounted four-cylinder in-line with belt-driven overhead camshaft, KKK turbocharger and Bosch K-Jetronic fuel injection. Bore × stroke 86.5 × 84.4 mm, displacement 1984 cc. Output 154.5 kW (210 bhp) @ 6000 rpm, torque 280 Nm (202 lb ft) @ 3500 rpm.

Transmission: Single-dry-plate clutch and five-speed manual gearbox, rear-mounted. Rear-wheel drive.

Suspension: Front, independent with MacPherson struts, coil springs, telescopic shock absorbers and anti-roll bar. Rear, independent with trailing arms, torsion bars, telescopic shock absorbers and anti-roll bar.

Steering: Rack and pinion.

Brakes: Ventilated discs front and rear, servo-assisted.

Tyres: 215/60 VR–15.

Dimensions: Length 4320 mm (170.1 in), width 1725 mm (67.9 in), height 1270 mm (50 in), wheelbase 2400 mm (94.5 in).

Unladen weight: 1000 kg (2204 lb).

Notes: Standard equipment includes electric window lifts, stereo radio/cassette player, tinted glass, electrically operated and heated outside mirror, headlamp washers and rear screen wash/wipe.

Identification: More powerful and more economical version of previous 911 SC model, also available with Targa bodywork incorporating removable roof panel.

Engine: Rear-mounted six-cylinder horizontally opposed with single chain-driven overhead camshafts and Bosch K-Jetronic fuel injection. Bore × stroke 95 × 70.4 mm, displacement 2994 cc. Output 152 kW (204 bhp) @ 5900 rpm, torque 264 Nm (195 lb ft) @ 4300 rpm.

Transmission: Single-dry-plate clutch and five-speed manual gearbox. Rear-wheel drive.

Suspension: Front, independent with MacPherson struts, torsion bars, telescopic shock absorbers and anti-roll bar. Rear, independent with trailing arms, torsion bars, telescopic shock absorbers and anti-roll bar.

Steering: Rack and pinion.

Brakes: Discs front and rear, servo-assisted.

Tyres: 185/70 VR–15 front, 215/60 VR–15 rear.

Dimensions: Length 4291 mm (168.9 in), width 1652 mm (65 in), height 1320 mm (52 in), wheelbase 2273 mm (89.5 in).

Unladen weight: 1160 kg (2557 lb).

Notes: Standard equipment includes stereo radio/cassette system, tinted and electrically operated windows and electric aerial.

PRINCESS (GB)

2000 HLS

Identification: High-specification Princess saloon with intermediate-size engine bridging gap between 1.7-litre four-cylinder and 2.2-litre six-cylinder models.

Engine: Front and transverse-mounted four-cylinder in-line with belt-driven overhead camshaft and SU carburettor. Bore × stroke 84.5 × 89 mm, displacement 1933 cc. Output 70 kW (93 bhp) @ 4900 rpm, torque 156 Nm (113 lb ft) @ 3400 rpm.

Transmission: Single-dry-plate clutch and four-speed manual gearbox, three-speed automatic transmission optional extra. Front-wheel drive.

Suspension: Front, independent with wishbones, Hydragas spring units and integral shock absorbers. Rear, independent with trailing arms, Hydragas spring units (linked to front units) and integral shock absorbers.

Steering: Rack and pinion, power-assistance optional extra.

Brakes: Discs front, drums rear, servo-assisted.

Tyres: 185/70 SR–14.

Dimensions: Length 4455 mm (175.4 in), width 1730 mm (68.1 in), height 1410 mm (55.5 in), wheelbase 2673 mm (105.3 in).

Unladen weight: 1215 kg (2678 lb).

Notes: Standard equipment includes tinted glass, vinyl roof, height-adjustable front seats and head restraints.

Identification: New convertible derivative of Scimitar GTE sports hatchback incorporating fixed roll-over hoop and powered by Ford Granada 2.8-litre engine.

Engine: Front-mounted V-6-cylinder with pushrod-operated overhead valves and Weber carburettor. Bore × stroke 93 × 68.5 mm, displacement 2792 cc. Output 101 kW (135 bhp) @ 5200 rpm, torque 220 Nm (159 lb ft) @ 3000 rpm.

Transmission: Single-dry-plate clutch and four-speed manual gearbox with overdrive on 3rd and 4th, three-speed automatic transmission optional extra. Rear-wheel drive.

Suspension: Front, independent with wishbones, coil springs, telescopic shock absorbers and anti-roll bar. Rear, live axle with trailing arms, Watt linkage, coil springs and telescopic shock absorbers.

Steering: Rack and pinion, power-assistance optional extra.

Brakes: Discs front, drums rear, servo-assisted.

Tyres: 185 HR–14.

Dimensions: Length 4432 mm (174.5 in), width 1720 mm (67.8 in), height 1321 mm (52 in), wheelbase 2637 mm (103.8 in).

Unladen weight: 1266 kg (2790 lb).

Notes: Standard equipment includes hood stowage cover, individually folding rear seats, velour-faced leathercloth upholstery and illuminated luggage compartment.

RELIANT (GB)   Scimitar GTE

Identification: Revised version of Scimitar sports hatchback, incorporating detail bodywork and suspension improvements and powered by Ford Granada 2.8-litre engine.

Engine: Front-mounted V-6-cylinder with pushrod-operated overhead valves and Weber carburettor. Bore × stroke 93 × 68.5 mm, displacement 2792 cc. Output 101 kW (135 bhp) @ 5200 rpm, torque 220 Nm (159 lb ft) @ 3000 rpm.

Transmission: Single-dry-plate clutch and four-speed manual gearbox with overdrive on 3rd and 4th, three-speed automatic transmission optional extra. Rear-wheel drive.

Suspension: Front, independent with wishbones, coil springs, telescopic shock absorbers and anti-roll bar. Rear, live axle with trailing arms, Watt linkage, coil springs and telescopic shock absorbers.

Steering: Rack and pinion, power-assistance optional extra.

Brakes: Discs front, drums rear, servo-assisted.

Tyres: 185 HR–14.

Dimensions: Length 4432 mm (174.5 in), width 1720 mm (67.8 in), height 1321 mm (52 in), wheelbase 2637 mm (103.8 in).

Unladen weight: 1311 kg (2890 lb).

Notes: Standard equipment includes rear screen wash/wipe, twin tailgate support struts, rear fog lamps and individually folding rear seats.

Identification: Higher-specification version of five-door saloon with 1.1-litre engine supplementing TL model with 845 cc power unit.

Engine: Front-mounted four-cylinder in-line with pushrod-operated overhead valves and Solex carburettor. Bore × stroke 70 × 72 mm, displacement 1108 cc. Output 25 kW (34 bhp) @ 4000 rpm, torque 77 Nm (55 lb ft) @ 2500 rpm.

Transmission: Single-dry-plate clutch and four-speed manual gearbox. Front-wheel drive.

Suspension: Front, independent with wishbones, torsion bars, telescopic shock absorbers and anti-roll bar. Rear, independent with trailing arms, torsion bars and telescopic shock absorbers.

Steering: Rack and pinion.

Brakes: Drums front and rear, servo-assisted.

Tyres: 135 SR–13.

Dimensions: Length 3668 mm (144.4 in), width 1509 mm (59.4 in), height 1549 mm (61 in), wheelbase 2400 mm (94.5 in).

Unladen weight: 720 kg (1586 lb).

Notes: Standard equipment includes reclining front seats, folding rear seats and parcels shelf, anti-theft steering lock and cloth-covered seats.

Identification: Larger-engined development of model originally offered with 956 cc engine and bridging gap between 845 cc base and 1.3-litre GTL models.

Engine: Front-mounted four-cylinder in-line with pushrod-operated overhead valves and Solex carburettor. Bore × stroke 70 × 72 mm, displacement 1108 cc. Output 33 kW (45 bhp) @ 4400 rpm, torque 88 Nm (63 lb ft) @ 2000 rpm.

Transmission: Single-dry-plate clutch and four-speed manual gearbox. Front-wheel drive.

Suspension: Front, independent with wishbones, torsion bars, telescopic shock absorbers and anti-roll bar. Rear, independent with trailing arms, torsion bars and telescopic shock absorbers.

Steering: Rack and pinion.

Brakes: Discs front, drums rear, servo-assisted.

Tyres: 135 SR–13.

Dimensions: Length 3493 mm (137.5 in), width 1524 mm (60 in), height 1397 mm (55 in), wheelbase 2400 mm (94.5 in).

Unladen weight: 775 kg (1708 lb).

Notes: Standard equipment includes cloth upholstery, two-speed wipers, folding rear seat and reclining front seats.

RENAULT (F) 5 Turbo

Identification: High-performance competition-orientated two-seater mid-engined coupe developed from Renault 5 body/chassis structure and powered by turbocharged version of Gordini engine.

Engine: Mid-mounted four-cylinder in-line with pushrod-operated overhead valves, Garrett AiResearch turbocharger and Bosch fuel injection. Bore × stroke 76 × 77 mm, displacement 1397 cc. Output 116 kW (160 bhp) @ 6000 rpm, torque 221 Nm (155 lb ft) @ 3250 rpm.

Transmission: Twin-plate clutch and five-speed manual gearbox. Rear-wheel drive.

Suspension: Front, independent with wishbones, torsion bars, telescopic shock absorbers and anti-roll bar. Rear, independent with wishbones, coil springs, telescopic shock absorbers and anti-roll bar.

Steering: Rack and pinion.

Brakes: Ventilated discs front and rear, servo-assisted.

Tyres: 190/55 HR–340 front, 220/55 VR–365 rear.

Dimensions: Length 3664 mm (144.3 in), width 1752 mm (69 in), height 1323 mm (52.1 in), wheelbase 2430 mm (95.7 in).

Unladen weight: 970 kg (2138 lb).

Notes: Standard equipment includes 10-gauge instrument panel, carpeted floor, engine cover and centre console. aerodynamic spoilers, alloy wheels, roof aerial and rear screen wash/wipe.

RENAULT (F)   Fuego GTL

Identification: Smallest-engined model in range of four-seater coupes offered in 1.4-litre, 1.6-litre and 2-litre engine sizes and supplementing similarly powered TL model.

Engine: Front-mounted four-cylinder in-line with pushrod-operated overhead valves and Solex carburettor. Bore × stroke 76 × 77 mm, displacement 1397 cc. Output 47 kW (64 bhp) @ 5500 rpm, torque 106 Nm (76 lb ft) @ 3000 rpm.

Transmission: Single-dry-plate clutch and four-speed manual gearbox, five-speed manual gearbox optional extra. Front-wheel drive.

Suspension: Front, independent with wishbones, coil springs, telescopic shock absorbers and anti-roll bar. Rear, dead axle with trailing arms, coil springs, telescopic shock absorbers and anti-roll bar.

Steering: Rack and pinion.

Brakes: Discs front, drums rear, servo-assisted.

Tyres: 175/70 SR–13.

Dimensions: Length 4360 mm (171.6 in), width 1690 mm (66.5 in), height 1315 mm (51.8 in), wheelbase 2445 mm (96.3 in).

Unladen weight: 1010 kg (2226 lb).

Notes: Standard equipment includes adjustable steering wheel, pantograph windscreen wipers, electric window lifts, front and rear spoilers and laminated screen.

Identification: Intermediate model in Fuego range spanning 1.4-litre, 1.6-litre and 2-litre engine sizes with choice of manual or automatic transmission.

Engine: Front-mounted four-cylinder in-line with pushrod-operated overhead valves and Solex carburettor. Bore × stroke 79 × 84 mm, displacement 1647 cc. Output 71 kW (96 bhp) @ 5750 rpm, torque 138 Nm (98 lb ft) @ 3500 rpm.

Transmission: Single-dry-plate clutch and five-speed manual gearbox, three-speed automatic transmission optional extra. Front-wheel drive.

Suspension: Front, independent with wishbones, coil springs, telescopic shock absorbers and anti-roll bar. Rear, dead axle with trailing arms, coil springs, telescopic shock absorbers and anti-roll bar.

Steering: Rack and pinion, power assistance optional extra.

Brakes: Discs front, drums rear, servo-assisted.

Tyres: 175/70 SR–13.

Dimensions: Length 4360 mm (171.6 in), width 1690 mm (66.5 in), height 1315 mm (51.8 in), wheelbase 2445 mm (96.3 in).

Unladen weight: 1035 kg (2281 lb).

Notes: Standard equipment includes halogen headlamps, electric window lifts, adjustable steering wheel and separately folding rear seats.

RENAULT (F)   18 TD

Identification: One of three diesel-engined additions to Renault 18 range supplementing 18 GTD saloon and 18 TD estate car and offering similar levels of trim as petrol-engined 18 TL and 18 GTL models.

Engine: Front-mounted four-cylinder in-line with belt-driven overhead camshaft and Bosch diesel injection. Bore × stroke 86 × 89 mm, displacement 2068 cc. Output 48 kW (66.5 bhp) @ 4500 rpm, torque 124 Nm (89 lb ft) @ 2250 rpm.

Transmission: Single-dry-plate clutch and four-speed manual gearbox. Front-wheel drive.

Suspension: Front, independent with wishbones, coil springs, telescopic shock absorbers and anti-roll bar. Rear, dead axle with trailing arms, coil springs, telescopic shock absorbers and anti-roll bar.

Steering: Rack and pinion.

Brakes: Discs front, drums rear, servo-assisted.

Tyres: 165 SR–13.

Dimensions: Length 4381 mm (172.5 in), width 1689 mm (66.5 in), height 1405 mm (55.3 in), wheelbase 2438 mm (96 in).

Unladen weight: 1050 kg (2314 lb).

Notes: Standard equipment includes reclining seats, cloth upholstery, centre console and two-speed wipers.

Identification: Turbocharged version of 1.6-litre 18 saloon with body changes including front and rear spoilers, special wheels and side decor plus uprated mechanical specification.

Engine: Front-mounted four-cylinder in-line with pushrod-operated overhead valves, Solex carburettor and Garrett exhaust-driven turbocharger. Bore × stroke 77 × 84 mm, displacement 1565 cc. Output 83 kW (110 bhp) @ 5000 rpm, torque 182 Nm (134 lb ft) @ 2250 rpm.

Transmission: Single-dry-plate clutch and five-speed manual gearbox. Front-wheel drive.

Suspension: Front, independent with wishbones, coil springs, telescopic shock absorbers and anti-roll bar. Rear, dead axle with trailing arms, coil springs, telescopic shock absorbers and anti-roll bar.

Steering: Rack and pinion, power-assisted.

Brakes: Ventilated discs front, drums rear, servo-assisted.

Tyres: 185/65 HR–14.

Dimensions: Length 4381 mm (172.5 in), width 1689 mm (66.5 in), height 1405 mm (55.3 in), wheelbase 2441 mm (96.1 in).

Unladen weight: 1040 kg (2292 lb).

Notes: Standard equipment includes alloy wheels, heavy-duty bumpers, velour upholstery, electric front window lifts, headlamp wash/wipe, adjustable head restraints and tinted glass.

Identification: Diesel-engined derivative of 2.1-litre petrol-engined Renault 20 with similar equipment specification to 20 TL model.

Engine: Front-mounted four-cylinder in-line with belt-driven overhead camshaft and Bosch diesel injection. Bore × stroke 86 × 89 mm, displacement 2068 cc. Output 46 kW (64 bhp) @ 4500 rpm, torque 127 Nm (94 lb ft) @ 2250 rpm.

Transmission: Single-dry-plate clutch and five-speed manual gearbox. Front-wheel drive.

Suspension: Front, independent with MacPherson struts, wishbones, coil springs, telescopic shock absorbers and anti-roll bar. Rear, independent with wishbones, coil springs, telescopic shock absorbers and anti-roll bar.

Steering: Rack and pinion.

Brakes: Ventilated discs front, drums rear, servo-assisted.

Tyres: 165 SR–13.

Dimensions: Length 4520 mm (178 in), width 1727 mm (68 in), height 1422 mm (56 in), wheelbase 2667 mm (105 in).

Unladen weight: 1260 kg (2777 lb).

Notes: Standard equipment includes fabric upholstery, centre console, reclining front seats, halogen headlamps with adjustment from driver's seat and transformable rear bench seat.

RENAULT (F)

20 TX

Identification: New top model of Renault 20 range featuring enlarged engine and completely restyled interior and supplementing TL, LS, TS, TD and GTD models.

Engine: Front-mounted four-cylinder in-line with belt-driven overhead camshaft and Weber carburettor. Bore × stroke 88 × 89 mm, displacement 2165 cc. Output 83 kW (115 bhp) @ 5500 rpm, torque 177 Nm (126 lb ft) @ 3000 rpm.

Transmission: Single-dry-plate clutch and five-speed manual gearbox, three-speed automatic transmission optional extra. Front-wheel drive.

Suspension: Front, independent with MacPherson struts, wishbones, coil springs and anti-roll bar. Rear, independent with wishbones, coil springs, telescopic shock absorbers and anti-roll bar.

Steering: Rack and pinion, power-assisted.

Brakes: Discs front, drums rear, servo-assisted.

Tyres: 175 HR-14.

Dimensions: Length 4520 mm (178 in), width 1727 mm (68 in), height 1422 mm (56 in), wheelbase 2667 mm (105 in).

Unladen weight: 1290 kg (2843 lb).

Notes: Standard equipment includes electric front window lifts, velour upholstery, front and rear head restraints and tinted glass.

RENAULT (F) 30 TX

Identification: Top model in Renault range, supplementing 30 TS and incorporating revised suspension linked to automatic light adjustment and completely changed interior.

Engine: Front-mounted V-6-cylinder with chain-driven overhead camshafts and Bosch K-Jetronic fuel injection. Bore × stroke 88 × 73 mm, displacement 2664 cc. Output 106 kW (142 bhp) @ 5500 rpm, torque 223 Nm (161 lb ft) @ 3000 rpm.

Transmission: Single-dry-plate clutch and five-speed manual gearbox or three-speed automatic transmission. Front-wheel drive.

Suspension: Front, independent with wishbones, coil springs, telescopic shock absorbers and anti-roll bar. Rear, independent with wishbones, coil springs, telescopic shock absorbers and anti-roll bar.

Steering: Rack and pinion, power-assisted.

Brakes: Ventilated discs front, discs rear, servo-assisted.

Tyres: 175 HR–14.

Dimensions: Length 4521 mm (178 in), width 1727 mm (68 in), height 1422 mm (56 in), wheelbase 2667 mm (105 in).

Unladen weight: 1340 kg (2954 lb).

Notes: Standard equipment includes electric sun roof, central door locking, headlamp wash/wipe, electric tailgate and fuel-filler flap release and alloy wheels.

ROLLS-ROYCE (GB)   Silver Spirit

Identification: Replacement model for Silver Shadow 2 four-door saloon incorporating completely restyled bodywork and revised rear suspension from Corniche and Camargue models.

Engine: Front-mounted V-8-cylinder with pushrod-operated overhead valves and twin SU carburettors. Bore × stroke 104.1 × 99.1 mm, displacement 6750 cc. Output and torque undisclosed.

Transmission: Three-speed automatic transmission. Rear-wheel drive.

Suspension: Front, independent with wishbones, coil springs, telescopic shock absorbers and anti-roll bar. Rear, independent with trailing arms, coil springs, auxiliary gas springs, strut-type shock absorbers and anti-roll bar. Self-levelling.

Steering: Rack and pinion, power-assisted.

Brakes: Ventilated discs front, discs rear, power-assisted.

Tyres: 235/70 HR–15.

Dimensions: 5278 mm (207.8 in), width 1887 mm (74.3 in), height 1485 mm (58.5 in), wheelbase 3061 mm (120.5 in).

Unladen weight: 2245 kg (4948 lb).

Notes: Standard equipment includes air-conditioning, headlamp wash/wipe, electrically operated gear selection, front seat adjustment, windows, mirrors, central door and boot locking, fuel-filler flap and aerial and stereo radio/cassette player with four speakers.

ROLLS-ROYCE (GB)　　　　Silver Spur

Identification: Long-wheelbase version of new four-door saloon replacing Silver Wraith 2 and incorporating completely restyled bodywork and revised rear suspension from Corniche and Camargue models.

Engine: Front-mounted V-8-cylinder with pushrod-operated overhead valves and twin SU carburettors. Bore × stroke 104.1 × 99.1 mm, displacement 6750 cc. Output and torque undisclosed.

Transmission: Three-speed automatic transmission. Rear-wheel drive.

Suspension: Front, independent with wishbones, coil springs, telescopic shock absorbers and anti-roll bar. Rear, independent with trailing arms, coil springs, auxiliary gas springs, strut-type shock absorbers and anti-roll bar. Self-levelling.

Steering: Rack and pinion, power-assisted.

Brakes: Ventilated discs front, discs rear, power-assisted.

Tyres: 235/70 HR-15.

Dimensions: Length 5370 mm (211.4 in), width 1887 mm (74.3 in), height 1485 mm (58.5 in), wheelbase 3160 mm (124.4 in).

Unladen weight: 2273 kg (5010 lb).

Notes: Standard equipment includes air-conditioning, headlamp wash/wipe, electrically operated gear selection, front seat adjustment, windows, mirrors, central door and boot locking, fuel-filler flap and aerial and stereo radio/cassette player with four speakers.

ROLLS-ROYCE (GB) Camargue

Identification: Top-of-the-range prestige two-door saloon with Pininfarina-styled bodywork offering four or five-seat accommodation and great luggage space.

Engine: Front-mounted V-8-cylinder with pushrod-operated overhead valves and twin SU carburettors. Bore × stroke 104.1 × 99.1 mm, displacement 6750 cc. Output and torque undisclosed.

Transmission: Three-speed automatic transmission. Rear-wheel drive.

Suspension: Front, independent with wishbones, coil springs, telescopic shock absorbers and anti-roll bar. Rear, independent with trailing arms, coil springs, auxiliary gas springs, strut-type shock absorbers and anti-roll bar. Self-levelling.

Steering: Rack and pinion, power-assisted.

Brakes: Ventilated discs front, discs rear, power-assisted.

Tyres: 235/70 HR–15.

Dimensions: Length 5170 mm (203.5 in), width 1920 mm (75.6 in), height 1470 mm (57.9 in), wheelbase 3050 mm (120.1 in).

Unladen weight: 2330 kg (5135 lb).

Notes: Standard equipment includes air-conditioning, cruise control, headlamp wash/wipe and all electrical equipment offered on Silver Spirit and Silver Spur models.

ROVER (GB) 2300 S

Identification: Additional model in revised SD1 range of five-door saloons, supplementing 2300 base model and offering more economical alternative to 2600 S with uprated specification.

Engine: Front-mounted six-cylinder in-line with belt-driven overhead camshaft and twin SU carburettors. Bore × stroke 81 × 76 mm, displacement 2350 cc. Output 92 kW (123 bhp) @ 5000 rpm, torque 182 Nm (134 lb ft) @ 4000 rpm.

Transmission: Single-dry-plate clutch and four-speed manual gearbox, three-speed automatic transmission or five-speed manual gearbox optional extra. Rear-wheel drive.

Suspension: Front, independent with MacPherson struts, coil springs, telescopic shock absorbers and anti-roll bar. Rear, live axle with torque tube, coil springs and telescopic shock absorbers.

Steering: Rack and pinion, power-assisted.

Brakes: Discs front, drums rear, servo-assisted.

Tyres: 175 HR–14.

Dimensions: Length 4698 mm (185 in), width 1768 mm (69.6 in), height 1382 mm (54.5 in), wheelbase 2815 mm (110.8 in).

Unladen weight: 1352 kg (2981 lb).

Notes: Standard equipment includes halogen headlamps, central door locking, carpeted luggage compartment, adjustable front seat lumbar support, full instrumentation and woven velvet upholstery.

ROVER (GB)

3500 SE

Identification: Uprated version of 3½-litre SD1 model with many detail improvements including revised interior trim and modified suspension to maintain level static ride height.

Engine: Front-mounted V-8-cylinder with pushrod-operated overhead valves and twin SU carburettors. Bore × stroke 88.9 × 71.1 mm, displacement 3528 cc. Output 116 kW (155 bhp) @ 5250 rpm, torque 268 Nm (198 lb ft) @ 2500 rpm.

Transmission: Single-dry-plate clutch and five-speed manual gearbox, three-speed automatic transmission optional extra. Rear-wheel drive.

Suspension: Front, independent with MacPherson struts, coil springs, telescopic shock absorbers and anti-roll bar. Rear, live axle with torque tube, coil springs and self-levelling/damper units.

Steering: Rack and pinion, power-assisted.

Brakes: Discs front, drums rear, servo-assisted.

Tyres: 195/70 HR–14.

Dimensions: Length 4698 mm (185 in), width 1768 mm (69.6 in), height 1382 mm (54.5 in), wheelbase 2815 mm (110.8 in).

Unladen weight: 1397 kg (3080 lb).

Notes: Standard equipment includes steel sun roof, alloy wheels, mudflaps, tinted glass, electric window lifts, central locking, radio/cassette player and twin halogen foglamps.

ROVER (GB)

Vanden Plas

Identification: New flagship of Rover range, replacing V8S and offering even higher level of equipment and appointments.

Engine: Front-mounted V-8-cylinder with pushrod-operated overhead valves and twin SU carburettors. Bore × stroke 88.9 × 71.1 mm, displacement 3528 cc. Output 116 kW (155 bhp) @ 5250 rpm, torque 268 Nm (198 lb ft) @ 2500 rpm.

Transmission: Single-dry-plate clutch and five-speed manual gearbox or three-speed automatic transmission. Rear-wheel drive.

Suspension: Front, independent with MacPherson struts, coil springs, telescopic shock absorbers and anti-roll bar. Rear, live axle with torque tube, coil springs and self-levelling/damper units.

Steering: Rack and pinion, power-assisted.

Brakes: Discs front, drums rear, servo-assisted.

Tyres: 195/70 HR-14.

Dimensions: Length 4698 mm (185 in), width 1768 mm (69.6 in), height 1382 mm (54.5 in), wheelbase 2815 mm (110.8 in).

Unladen weight: 1404 kg (3097 lb).

Notes: Standard equipment includes cruise control, machined and painted alloy wheels, leather upholstery, headlamp power wash, stereo radio/cassette player, electric steel sun roof, bronze tinted glass, front and rear head restraints with cushions and shag pile foot well mats.

Identification: Four-door saloon version of 900 GLs five-door hatchback, supplementing GLE and Turbo versions.

Engine: Front-mounted four-cylinder in-line with chain-driven overhead camshaft and twin Zenith-Stromberg carburettors. Bore × stroke 90 × 78 mm, displacement 1985 cc. Output 81 kW (108 bhp) @ 5200 rpm, torque 167 Nm (121 lb ft) @ 3300 rpm.

Transmission: Single-dry-plate clutch and four-speed manual gearbox, three-speed automatic transmission optional extra. Front-wheel drive.

Suspension: Front, independent with wishbones, coil springs and telescopic shock absorbers. Rear, dead axle with four links, Panhard rod, coil springs and telescopic shock absorbers.

Steering: Rack and pinion, power-assisted.

Brakes: Discs front and rear, servo-assisted.

Tyres: 165 SR–15.

Dimensions: Length 4740 mm (186.6 in), width 1690 mm (66.5 in), height 1420 mm (55.9 in), wheelbase 2525 mm (99.4 in).

Unladen weight: 1216 kg (2860 lb).

Notes: Standard equipment includes heated driver's and front passenger's seats, electric front windows and adjustable head restraints.

SAAB (S)   900 GLE Saloon

Identification: Four-door saloon version of intermediate 900 model bridging gap between GLs and Turbo models and supplementing five-door hatchback version.

Engine: Front-mounted four-cylinder in-line with chain-driven overhead camshaft and Bosch fuel injection. Bore × stroke 90 × 78 mm, displacement 1985 cc. Output 88 kW (118 bhp) @ 5500 rpm, torque 170 Nm (123 lb ft) @ 3700 rpm.

Transmission: Single-dry-plate clutch and five-speed manual gearbox, three-speed automatic transmission optional extra. Front-wheel drive.

Suspension: Front, independent with wishbones, coil springs and telescopic shock absorbers. Rear, dead axle with four links, Panhard rod, coil springs and telescopic shock absorbers.

Steering: Rack and pinion, power-assisted.

Brakes: Discs front and rear, servo-assisted.

Tyres: 175/70 HR–15.

Dimensions: Length 4740 mm (186.6 in), width 1690 mm (66.5 in), height 1420 mm (55.9 in), wheelbase 2525 mm (99.4 in).

Unladen weight: 1257 kg (2770 lb).

Notes: Standard equipment includes electrically operated exterior rear-view mirrors and front door windows, and heated driver's and front passenger's seats.

SAAB (S)   900 Turbo 3-door

Identification: Intermediate of three turbocharged SAAB saloons bridging gap between three-door 99 Turbo and five-door 900 Turbo and supplementing similarly bodied GLs and EMS saloons.

Engine: Front-mounted four-cylinder in-line with chain-driven overhead camshaft, exhaust-driven turbocharger and Bosch fuel injection. Bore × stroke 90 × 78 mm, displacement 1985 cc. Output 108 kW (145 bhp) @ 5000 rpm, torque 240 Nm (174 lb ft) @ 3000 rpm.

Transmission: Single-dry-plate clutch and five-speed manual gearbox. Front-wheel drive.

Suspension: Front, independent with wishbones, coil springs and telescopic shock absorbers. Rear, dead axle with four links, Panhard rod, coil springs and telescopic shock absorbers.

Steering: Rack and pinion, power-assisted.

Brakes: Discs front and rear, servo-assisted.

Tyres: 195/60 HR–15.

Dimensions: Length 4739 mm (186.6 in), width 1690 mm (66.5 in), height 1420 mm (55.9 in), wheelbase 2525 mm (99.4 in).

Unladen weight: 1185 kg (2612 lb).

Notes: Standard equipment includes halogen headlamps, headlamp wipers, anti-theft gear lock, tinted glass, heated driver's seat and electrically controlled rear-view mirrors.

SAAB (S)   900 Turbo Saloon

Identification: Four-door saloon version of 900 Turbo with conventional luggage compartment offered as alternative to five-door model.

Engine: Front-mounted four-cylinder in-line with chain-driven overhead camshaft, exhaust-driven turbocharger and Bosch fuel injection. Bore × stroke 90 × 78 mm, displacement 1985 cc. Output 108 kW (145 bhp) @ 5000 rpm, torque 240 Nm (174 lb ft) @ 3000 rpm.

Transmission: Single-dry-plate clutch and five-speed manual gearbox. Front-wheel drive.

Suspension: Front, independent with wishbones, coil springs and telescopic shock absorbers. Rear, dead axle with four links, Panhard rod, coil springs and telescopic shock absorbers.

Steering: Rack and pinion, power-assisted.

Brakes: Discs front and rear, servo-assisted.

Tyres: 180/65 HR–390.

Dimensions: Length 4740 mm (186.6 in), width 1690 mm (66.5 in), height 1420 mm (55.9 in), wheelbase 2525 mm (99.4 in).

Unladen weight: 1280 kg (2820 lb).

Notes: Standard equipment includes folding rear seat, halogen headlamps, anti-theft gear lock, tinted glass, heated front seats and electrically controlled rear-view mirrors.

SKODA (CS) 120LSE Super Estelle

Identification: Top model in range of rear-engined saloons supplementing 1-litre 105S and 105L and 1.2-litre 120 L, 120LE, and 120LS models.

Engine: Rear-mounted four-cylinder in-line with pushrod-operated overhead valves and Jikov carburettor. Bore × stroke 72 × 72 mm, displacement 1174 cc. Output 43 kW (58 bhp) @ 5200 rpm, torque 90 Nm (67 lb ft) @ 3250 rpm.

Transmission: Single-dry-plate clutch and four-speed manual gearbox. Rear-wheel drive.

Suspension: Front, independent with wishbones, coil springs, telescopic shock absorbers and anti-roll bar. Rear, independent with swing-axles, leading arms, coil springs and telescopic shock absorbers.

Steering: Screw and nut.

Brakes: Discs front, drums rear, servo-assisted.

Tyres: 165 SR–13.

Dimensions: Length 4160 mm (163.8 in), width 1595 mm (62.8 in), height 1400 mm (55.1 in), wheelbase 2400 mm (94.5 in).

Unladen weight: 885 kg (1951 lb).

Notes: Standard equipment includes tilt/lift-out sun roof, dual headlamps, rev counter, vinyl roof, sports gear shift and radio/cassette player.

SUBARU (J)   1600 GFT Hardtop

Identification: Additional two-door four-seater model to Subaru range with uprated 1.6-litre engine and five-speed transmission.

Engine: Front-mounted four-cylinder horizontally opposed with pushrod-operated overhead valves and twin Hitachi carburettors. Bore × stroke 92 × 60 mm, displacement 1595 cc. Output 63 kW (85 bhp) @ 6000 rpm. torque 115 Nm (83 lb ft) @ 4000 rpm.

Transmission: Single-dry-plate clutch and five-speed manual gearbox. Front-wheel drive.

Suspension: Front, independent with MacPherson struts, coil springs, telescopic shock absorbers and anti-roll bar. Rear independent with semi-trailing arms, torsion bars and telescopic shock absorbers.

Steering: Rack and pinion.

Brakes: Discs front, drums rear, servo-assisted.

Tyres: 175/70 HR-13.

Dimensions: Length 4155 mm (163.6 in), width 1615 mm (63.6 in), height 1350 mm (53.1 in), wheelbase 2460 mm (96.8 in).

Unladen weight: 905 kg (1995 lb).

Notes: Standard equipment includes radio, quartz digital clock, tinted glass, reclining front seats and adjustable head restraints.

SUBARU (J)   1600 4WD Estate

Identification: Addition to range of four-wheel-drive passenger vehicles supplementing 1600 4WD saloon, also available in two-wheel-drive form as 1600 DL.

Engine: Front-mounted four-cylinder horizontally opposed with pushrod-operated overhead valves and Hitachi carburettor. Bore × stroke 92 × 60 mm, displacement 1595 cc. Output 53 kW (71 bhp) @ 5200 rpm, torque 115 Nm (83 lb ft) @ 2400 rpm.

Transmission: Single-dry-plate clutch and four-speed manual gearbox. Front-wheel or four-wheel drive.

Suspension: Front, independent with MacPherson struts, coil springs, telescopic shock absorbers and anti-roll bar. Rear, independent with semi-trailing arms, torsion bars and telescopic shock absorbers.

Steering: Rack and pinion.

Brakes: Discs front, drums rear, servo-assisted.

Tyres: 155R–13C–6PR.

Dimensions: Length 4275 mm (168.3 in), width 1620 mm (63.8 in), height 1445 mm (56.9 in), wheelbase 2445 mm (96.3 in).

Unladen weight: 1010 kg (2227 lb).

Notes: Standard equipment includes reclining seats, radio, tinted glass, rear screen wash/wipe and quartz digital clock.

Identification: Top of Horizon range of front-wheel-drive five-door hatchback saloons with high level of equipment including larger engine and automatic transmission.

Engine: Front and transverse-mounted four-cylinder in-line with pushrod-operated overhead valves and Weber carburettor. Bore × stroke 76.7 × 78 mm, displacement 1442 cc. Output 61 kW (82 bhp) @ 5600 rpm, torque 123 Nm (91 lb ft) @ 3000 rpm.

Transmission: Three-speed automatic transmission. Front-wheel drive.

Suspension: Front, independent with wishbones, torsion bars, telescopic shock absorbers and anti-roll bar. Rear, independent with trailing arms, transverse torsion bars, telescopic shock absorbers and anti-roll bar.

Steering: Rack and pinion.

Brakes: Discs front, drums rear, servo-assisted.

Tyres: 155 SR–13.

Dimensions: Length 3960 mm (155.9 in), width 1680 mm (66.1 in), height 1410 mm (55.5 in), wheelbase 2520 mm (99.2 in).

Unladen weight: 1025 kg (2259 lb).

Notes: Standard equipment includes trip computer, cruise control, tailgate wash/wipe, front and rear head restraints, tinted glass, laminated screen and radio/cassette player.

TALBOT (F)   Matra Rancho

Identification: Improved version of multi-purpose leisure vehicle incorporating additional rear-facing seats, tartan cloth seat inserts and improved detail equipment.

Engine: Front-mounted four-cylinder in-line with pushrod-operated overhead valves and Weber carburettor. Bore × stroke 76.7 × 78 mm, displacement 1442 cc. Output 60 kW (80 bhp) @ 5600 rpm, torque 122 Nm (88 lb ft) @ 3000 rpm.

Transmission: Single-dry-plate clutch and four-speed manual gearbox. Front-wheel drive.

Suspension: Front, independent with wishbones, torsion bars, telescopic shock absorbers and anti-roll bar. Rear, independent with trailing arms, torsion bars, telescopic shock absorbers and anti-roll bar.

Steering: Rack and pinion.

Brakes: Discs front, drums rear, servo-assisted.

Tyres: 185/70 HR–14.

Dimensions: Length 4315 mm (169.9 in), width 1692 mm (66.6 in), height 1735 mm (68.3 in), wheelbase 2520 mm (99.2 in).

Unladen weight: 1140 kg (2513 lb).

Notes: Standard equipment includes integral roof rack, towing hitch, auxiliary lamps, laminated screen, tinted glass and push-button radio.

Identification: Intermediate model in revised range of three-door hatchback saloons bridging gap between 1.0-litre and 1.6-litre models with LS, GL and GLS trim levels.

Engine: Front-mounted four-cylinder in-line with pushrod-operated overhead valves and Zenith carburettor. Bore × stroke 78.6 × 66.7 mm, displacement 1295 cc. Output 44 kW (59 bhp) @ 5000 rpm, torque 94 Nm (69 lb ft) @ 2600 rpm.

Transmission: Single-dry-plate clutch and four-speed manual gearbox, three-speed automatic transmission optional extra. Rear-wheel drive.

Suspension: Front, independent with MacPherson struts, coil springs, telescopic shock absorbers and anti-roll bar. Rear, live axle with trailing arms, coil springs and telescopic shock absorbers.

Steering: Rack and pinion.

Brakes: Discs front, drums rear, servo-assisted.

Tyres: 155 SR–13.

Dimensions: Length 3829 mm (150.7 in), width 1603 mm (63.1 in), height 1394 mm (54.9 in), wheelbase 2413 mm (95 in).

Unladen weight: 890 kg (1962 lb).

Notes: Standard equipment includes fabric upholstery, head restraints, radio, split rear seat squab, centre console and rear parcels shelf.

TALBOT (GB)   Avenger GLS Estate

Identification: Additional model at top end of Avenger estate range supplementing 1.3-litre and 1.6-litre LS and GL models.

Engine: Front-mounted four-cylinder in-line with pushrod-operated overhead valves and Zenith carburettor. Bore × stroke 87.4 × 66.7 mm, displacement 1598 cc. Output 59 kW (80 bhp) @ 5400 rpm, torque 120 Nm (86 lb ft) @ 4400 rpm.

Transmission: Single-dry-plate clutch and four-speed manual gearbox, three-speed automatic transmission optional extra. Rear-wheel drive.

Suspension: Front, independent with MacPherson struts, coil springs, telescopic shock absorbers and anti-roll bar. Rear, live axle with trailing arms, coil springs and telescopic shock absorbers.

Steering: Rack and pinion.

Brakes: Discs front, drums rear, servo-assisted.

Tyres: 155 SR–13.

Dimensions: Length 4272 mm (168.2 in), width 1613 mm (63.5 in), height 1415 mm (55.7 in), wheelbase 2489 mm (98 in).

Unladen weight: 980 kg (2160 lb).

Notes: Standard equipment includes chromed roof rack, halogen headlamps, front fog lamps, reversing lamps and radio/stereo cassette player.

TALBOT (GB)   Alpine 1600 SX

Identification: New top model in Alpine range of five-door hatchbacks with revised front-end styling and supplementing LS, GL and GLS models.

Engine: Front and transverse-mounted four-cylinder in-line with pushrod-operated overhead valves and Weber carburettor. Bore × stroke 80.6 × 78 mm, displacement 1592 cc. Output 64 kW (87 bhp) @ 5400 rpm, torque 134 Nm (96 lb ft) @ 3000 rpm.

Transmission: Three-speed automatic transmission. Front-wheel drive.

Suspension: Front, independent with wishbones, torsion bars and anti-roll bar. Rear, independent with trailing arms, coil springs, telescopic shock absorbers and anti-roll bar.

Steering: Rack and pinion, power-assisted.

Brakes: Discs front, drums rear, servo-assisted.

Tyres: 165 SR–13.

Dimensions: Length 4318 mm (170 in), width 1680 mm (66.1 in), height 1390 mm (54.7 in), wheelbase 2604 mm (102.5 in).

Unladen weight: 1110 kg (2447 lb).

Notes: Standard equipment includes rear screen and headlamp wash/wipe, radio/stereo cassette player, electric front window lifts, central door locking, trip computer and velour upholstery.

Identification: Intermediate model of new range of four-door saloons based on Alpine hatchback with choice of 1.3-litre and two 1.6-litre engines and four-speed or five-speed gearbox.

Engine: Front and transverse-mounted four-cylinder in-line with pushrod-operated overhead valves and Solex carburettor. Bore × stroke 80.6 × 78 mm, displacement 1592 cc. Output 53 kW (72 bhp) @ 5200 rpm, torque 134 Nm (96 lb ft) @ 3000 rpm.

Transmission: Single-dry-plate clutch and four-speed manual gearbox, three-speed automatic transmission optional extra. Front-wheel drive.

Suspension: Front, independent with wishbones, torsion bars, telescopic shock absorbers and anti-roll bar. Rear, independent with semi-trailing arms, coil springs, telescopic shock absorbers and anti-roll bar.

Steering: Rack and pinion.

Brakes: Discs front, drums rear, servo-assisted.

Dimensions: Length 4393 mm (173 in), width 1680 mm (66 in), height 1390 mm (54.7 in), wheelbase 2604 mm (102.5 in).

Unladen weight: 1024 kg (2257 lb).

Notes: Standard equipment includes halogen headlamps, front seat head restraints, stainless steel trim mouldings, fabric interior trim and illuminated luggage compartment.

Identification: Top model in Solara range, supplementing LS, GL and GLS models and equipped with automatic transmission.

Engine: Front and transverse-mounted four-cylinder in-line with pushrod-operated overhead valves and twin-choke Weber carburettor. Bore × stroke 80.6 × 78 mm, displacement 1592 cc. Output 64 kW (87 bhp) @ 5400 rpm, torque 141 Nm (101 lb ft) @ 3000 rpm.

Transmission: Three-speed automatic transmission. Front-wheel drive.

Suspension: Front, independent with wishbones, torsion bars, telescopic shock absorbers and anti-roll bar. Rear, independent with semi-trailing arms, coil springs, telescopic shock absorbers and anti-roll bar.

Steering: Rack and pinion, power-assisted.

Brakes: Discs front, drums rear, servo-assisted.

Tyres: 165 SR–13.

Dimensions: Length 4393 mm (173 in), width 1680 mm (66 in), height 1390 mm (54.7 in), wheelbase 2604 mm (102.5 in).

Unladen weight: 1096 kg (2416 lb).

Notes: Standard equipment includes alloy wheels, velour upholstery, headlamp wash/wipe, on-board computer recording time, distance, speed and consumption, central door locking and cruise control.

Identification: Improved version of 1.2-litre Starlet five-door saloon with revised front and rear styling and uprated interior specification.

Engine: Front-mounted four-cylinder in-line with pushrod-operated overhead valves and Aisan carburettor. Bore × stroke 75 × 66 mm, displacement 1166 cc. Output 42 kW (56 bhp) @ 6000 rpm, torque 86 Nm (62 lb ft) @ 3800 rpm.

Transmission: Single-dry-plate clutch and five-speed manual gearbox. Rear-wheel drive.

Suspension: Front, independent with MacPherson struts, coil springs, telescopic shock absorbers and integral anti-roll bar. Rear, live axle with four links, Panhard rod, coil springs and telescopic shock absorbers.

Steering: Rack and pinion.

Brakes: Discs front, drums rear, servo-assisted.

Tyres: 145 SR–13.

Dimensions: Length 3725 mm (146.7 in), width 1532 mm (60.3 in), height 1380 mm (54.3 in), wheelbase 2300 mm (90.6 in).

Unladen weight: 725 kg (1600 lb).

Notes: Standard equipment includes fabric upholstery, split rear seat backs, rear screen wash/wipe, tinted glass and pushbutton radio.

TOYOTA (J)

Starlet 1200 S

Identification: Sporting model of Starlet range, supplementing 1-litre-engined three-door saloon and incorporating latest exterior styling changes plus uprated interior specification.

Engine: Front-mounted four-cylinder in-line with pushrod-operated overhead valves and Aisan carburettor. Bore × stroke 75 × 66 mm, displacement 1166 cc. Output 42 kW (56 bhp) @ 6000 rpm, torque 86 Nm (62 lb ft) @ 3800 rpm.

Transmission: Single-dry-plate clutch and five-speed manual gearbox. Rear-wheel drive.

Suspension: Front, independent with MacPherson struts, coil springs, telescopic shock absorbers and integral anti-roll bar. Rear, live axle with four links, Panhard rod, coil springs and telescopic shock absorbers.

Steering: Rack and pinion.

Brakes: Discs front, drums rear, servo-assisted.

Tyres: 165/70 SR–13.

Dimensions: Length 3725 mm (146.7 in), width 1532 mm (60.3 in), height 1380 mm (54.3 in), wheelbase 2300 mm (90.6 in).

Unladen weight: 755 kg (1665 lb).

Notes: Standard equipment includes fabric upholstery, split rear seat backs, rear screen wash/wipe, tinted glass and pushbutton radio.

TOYOTA (J)　　　　Corolla 1300 4-door

Identification: Intermediate model in 1.3-litre restyled Corolla range supplementing two-door saloon and five-door estate car models.

Engine: Front-mounted four-cylinder in-line with pushrod-operated overhead valves and Aisan carburettor. Bore × stroke 75 × 73 mm, displacement 1290 cc. Output 43 kW (59 bhp) @ 5600 rpm, torque 95 Nm (68 lb ft) @ 3600 rpm.

Transmission: Single-dry-plate clutch and four-speed manual gearbox, two-speed automatic transmission optional extra. Rear-wheel drive.

Suspension: Front, independent with MacPherson struts, coil springs, telescopic shock absorbers and anti-roll bar. Rear, live axle with four links, Panhard rod, coil springs and telescopic shock absorbers.

Steering: Rack and pinion.

Brakes: Discs front, drums rear, servo-assisted.

Tyres: 155 SR–13.

Dimensions: Length 4050 mm (159.5 in), width 1610 mm (63.4 in), height 1395 mm (54.9 in), wheelbase 2400 mm (94.5 in).

Unladen weight: 855 kg (1885 lb).

Notes: Standard equipment includes electric radiator fan, radio and fabric upholstery.

TOYOTA (J)   Corolla 1600 Liftback

Identification: Three-door sporting hatchback alternative to two-door and four-door Corolla saloons with larger 1.6-litre engine.

Engine: Front-mounted four-cylinder in-line with pushrod-operated overhead valves and Aisan carburettor. Bore × stroke 85 × 70 mm, displacement 1588 cc. Output 54 kW (74 bhp) @ 5200 rpm, torque 118 Nm (84 lb ft) @ 3800 rpm.

Transmission: Single-dry-plate clutch and four-speed manual gearbox. Rear-wheel drive.

Suspension: Front, independent with MacPherson struts, coil springs, telescopic shock absorbers and anti-roll bar. Rear, live axle with four links, Panhard rod, coil springs and telescopic shock absorbers.

Steering: Recirculating ball.

Brakes: Discs front, drums rear, servo-assisted.

Tyres: 165 SR–13.

Dimensions: Length 4105 mm (161.6 in), width 1625 mm (64 in), height 1340 mm (52.8 in), wheelbase 2400 mm (94.5 in).

Unladen weight: 890 kg (2070 lb)

Notes: Standard equipment includes striped fabric upholstery, individually folding rear seats, tailgate wash/wipe and frameless door windows.

TOYOTA (J)　　　Corolla 1600 Coupe

Identification: Highest-performance model in restyled Corolla range featuring three-door bodywork, 1.6-litre engine and five-speed transmission.

Engine: Front-mounted four-cylinder in-line with pushrod-operated overhead valves and twin Aisan carburettors. Bore × stroke 85 × 70 mm, displacement 1588 cc. Output 63 kW (85 bhp) @ 5600 rpm, torque 125 Nm (89 lb ft) @ 4000 rpm.

Transmission: Single-dry-plate clutch and five-speed manual gearbox. Rear-wheel drive.

Suspension: Front, independent with MacPherson struts, coil springs, telescopic shock absorbers and anti-roll bar. Rear, live axle with four links, Panhard rod, coil springs and telescopic shock absorbers.

Steering: Recirculating ball.

Brakes: Discs front, drums rear, servo-assisted.

Tyres: 185/70 HR–13.

Dimensions: Length 4105 mm (161.6 in), width 1625 mm (64 in), height 1335 mm (52.6 in), wheelbase 2400 mm (94.5 in).

Unladen weight: 950 kg (2095 lb).

Notes: Standard equipment includes striped fabric upholstery, individually folding rear seats, tailgate wash/wipe and digital quartz clock.

TOYOTA (J)   Carina 1600 Saloon

Identification: Revised version of 1.6-litre saloon with rede-signed front and rear styling and substantially improved noise suppression.

Engine: Front-mounted four-cylinder in-line with pushrod-op-erated overhead valves and Aisan carburettor. Bore × stroke 85 × 70 mm, displacement 1588 cc. Output 53 kW (72 bhp) @ 5200 rpm, torque 118 Nm (84 lb ft) @ 3800 rpm.

Transmission: Single-dry-plate clutch and four-speed manual gearbox, three-speed automatic transmission optional extra. Rear-wheel drive.

Suspension: Front, independent with MacPherson struts, coil springs, telescopic shock absorbers and anti-roll bar. Rear, live axle with four links, Panhard rod, coil springs and telescopic shock absorbers.

Steering: Recirculating ball.

Brakes: Discs front, drums rear, servo-assisted.

Tyres: 165 SR–13.

Dimensions: 4330 mm (170.5 in), width 1620 mm (64.2 in), height 1394 mm (54.9 in), wheelbase 2500 mm (98.4 in).

Unladen weight: 980 kg (2160 lb).

Notes: Standard equipment includes fabric upholstery, rear fog lamp, adjustable head restraints and halogen headlamps.

TOYOTA (J)   Carina 1600 Estate

Identification: Estate car alternative to four-door Carina saloon with different rear suspension and restricted to manual transmission.

Engine: Front-mounted four-cylinder in-line with pushrod-operated overhead valves and Aisan carburettor. Bore × stroke 85 × 70 mm, displacement 1588 cc. Output 53 kW (72 bhp) @ 5200 rpm, torque 118 Nm (84 lb ft) @ 3800 rpm.

Transmission: Single-dry-plate clutch and four-speed manual gearbox. Rear-wheel drive.

Suspension: Front, independent with MacPherson struts, coil springs, telescopic shock absorbers and anti-roll bar. Rear, live axle with semi-elliptic springs and telescopic shock absorbers.

Steering: Recirculating ball.

Brakes: Discs front, drums rear, servo-assisted.

Tyres: 165 SR–13.

Dimensions: Length 4370 mm (172 in), width 1630 mm (64.2 in), height 1400 mm (55.1 in), wheelbase 2494 mm (98.2 in).

Unladen weight: 1005 kg (2115 lb).

Notes: Standard equipment includes fabric upholstery, rear fog lamp, adjustable head restraints and halogen headlamps.

TOYOTA (J)   Celica 1600 ST Coupe

Identification: Improved coupe version of 1.6-litre Celica with new front and rear styling incorporating dual rectangular headlamps and separate rear fog lamp.

Engine: Front-mounted four-cylinder in-line with pushrod-operated overhead valves, and twin Aisan carburettors. Bore × stroke 85 × 70 mm, displacement 1588 cc. Output 63 kW (85 bhp) @ 5600 rpm, torque 125 Nm (89 lb ft) @ 4000 rpm.

Transmission: Single-dry-plate clutch and five-speed manual gearbox. Rear-wheel drive.

Suspension: Front, independent with MacPherson struts, coil springs, telescopic shock absorbers and anti-roll bar. Rear, live axle with four links, Panhard rod, coil springs and telescopic shock absorbers.

Steering: Recirculating ball.

Brakes: Discs front, drums rear, servo-assisted.

Tyres: 165 SR-13.

Dimensions: Length 4305 mm (169.5 in), width 1636 mm (64.4 in), height 1320 mm (52 in), wheelbase 2500 mm (98.4 in).

Unladen weight: 995 kg (2195 lb).

Notes: Standard equipment includes height-adjustable driver's seat, choke warning light and front air dam incorporating brake-cooling duct.

TOYOTA (J)   Celica 2000 XT Liftback

Identification: Intermediate model in range of restyled 2-litre three-door Celicas bridging gap between 2000 ST and twin-overhead-camshaft 2000 GT.

Engine: Front-mounted four-cylinder in-line with belt-driven overhead camshaft and Nikki carburettor. Bore × stroke 88.5 × 80 mm, displacement 1968 cc. Output 67 kW (89 bhp) @ 5000 rpm, torque 148 Nm (107 lb ft) @ 3600 rpm.

Transmission: Single-dry-plate clutch and five-speed manual gearbox, three-speed automatic transmission optional extra. Rear-wheel drive.

Suspension: Front, independent with MacPherson struts, coil springs, telescopic shock absorbers and anti-roll bar. Rear, live axle with four links, Panhard rod, coil springs and telescopic shock absorbers.

Steering: Recirculating ball.

Brakes: Discs front, drums rear, servo-assisted.

Tyres: 185/70 HR–14.

Dimensions: Length 4330 mm (170.5 in), width 1640 mm (64.6 in), height 1320 mm (52 in), wheelbase 2500 mm (98.4 in).

Unladen weight: 1055 kg (2325 lb).

Notes: Standard equipment includes tilting front seats with memory for correct return postion, left foot rest and interior light delay switch.

TOYOTA (J)   Crown Super 2.8

Identification: New executive flagship of Toyota range with restyled bodywork, larger engine and overdrive-automatic transmission.

Engine: Front-mounted six-cylinder in-line with chain-driven overhead camshaft and Bosch fuel injection. Bore × stroke 83 × 85 mm, displacement 2759 cc. Output 107 kW (145 bhp) @ 5000 rpm, torque 230 Nm (167 lb ft) @ 4000 rpm.

Transmission: Three-speed automatic transmission with manual overdrive. Rear-wheel drive.

Suspension: Front, independent with wishbones, coil springs, telescopic shock absorbers and anti-roll bar. Rear, live axle with four links, coil springs, Panhard rod, telescopic shock absorbers and anti-roll bar.

Steering: Recirculating ball, power-assisted.

Brakes: Discs front, drums rear, servo-assisted.

Tyres: 195/70 HR–14.

Dimensions: Length 4860 mm (191.3 in), width 1690 mm (66.5 in), height 1475 mm (58.1 in), wheelbase 2690 mm (105.9 in).

Unladen weight: 1435 kg (3165 lb).

Notes: Standard equipment includes front and rear adjustable head restraints, air-conditioning, electric window lifts, stereo radio/cassette player with four speakers, electric luggage compartment and fuel-filler release and cut-pile carpeting.

Identification: Open-topped version of TR7 coupe incorporating body changes to rear deck and new front spoiler and European mechanical specification.

Engine: Front-mounted four-cylinder in-line with chain-driven overhead camshaft and twin Zenith carburettors. Bore × stroke 90.3 × 78 mm, displacement 1998 cc. Output 78 kW (105 bhp) @ 5500 rpm, torque 161 Nm (119 lb ft) @ 3500 rpm.

Transmission: Single-dry-plate clutch and five-speed manual gearbox, three-speed automatic transmission optional extra. Rear-wheel drive.

Suspension: Front, independent with MacPherson struts, coil springs, telescopic shock absorbers and anti-roll bar. Rear, live axle with four links, coil springs, telescopic shock absorbers and anti-roll bar.

Steering: Rack and pinion.

Brakes: Discs front, drums rear, servo-assisted.

Tyres: 185/70 HR-13 (175/70 HR—13 with automatic transmission).

Dimensions: Length 4065 mm (160 in), width 1681 mm (66.2 in), height 1257 mm (49.5 in), wheelbase 2160 mm (85 in).

Unladen weight: 1066 kg (2350 lb).

Notes: Standard equipment includes hood with detachable zipped rear panel, rear fog lamps, full carpeting and plaid-patterned fabric upholstery.

TVR (GB)

Tasmin

Identification: Completely new two-seater coupe incorporating glass-fibre bodywork on multi-tubular steel chassis and powered by Ford Granada engine.

Engine: Front-mounted V-6-cylinder with pushrod-operated overhead valves and Bosch K-Jetronic fuel injection. Bore × stroke 93 × 68.5 mm, displacement 2792 cc. Output 120 kW (160 bhp) @ 5700 rpm, torque 224 Nm (162 lb ft) @ 4300 rpm.

Transmission: Single-dry-plate clutch and four-speed manual gearbox. Rear-wheel drive.

Suspension: Front, independent with wishbones, coil springs, telescopic shock absorbers and anti-roll bar. Rear, independent with trailing arms, fixed-length drive shafts, coil springs and telescopic shock absorbers.

Steering: Rack and pinion.

Brakes: Discs front and rear, servo-assisted.

Tyres: 205/60 VR–14.

Dimensions: Length 4013 mm (158 in), width 1727 mm (68 in), height 1191 mm (46.9 in), wheelbase 2388 mm (94 in).

Unladen weight: 1050 kg (2314 lb).

Notes: Standard equipment includes electric window lifts, stereo radio/cassette player, velour-trimmed upholstery and carpeted luggage area.

Identification: Two-plus-two derivative of Tasmin two-seater coupe with shorter front deck and lengthened passenger compartment.

Engine: Front-mounted V-6-cylinder with pushrod-operated overhead valves and Bosch K-Jetronic fuel injection. Bore × stroke 93 × 68.5 mm, displacement 2792 cc. Output 120 kW (160 bhp) @ 5700 rpm, torque 224 Nm (162 lb ft) @ 4300 rpm.

Transmission: Single-dry-plate clutch and four-speed manual gearbox, three-speed automatic transmission optional extra. Rear-wheel drive.

Suspension: Front, independent with wishbones, coil springs, telescopic shock absorbers and anti-roll bar. Rear, independent with trailing arms, fixed-length drive shafts, coil springs and telescopic shock absorbers.

Steering: Rack and pinion.

Brakes: Discs front and rear, servo-assisted.

Tyres: 205/60 VR–14.

Dimensions: Length 4080 mm (161 in), width 1728 mm (68 in), height 1192 mm (47 in), wheelbase 2387 mm (94 in).

Unladen weight: Approx. 1075 kg (2369 lb).

Notes: Standard equipment includes tinted glass, laminated screen, adjustable head restraints and velour-trimmed upholstery.

TVR (GB)　　　　　　　Tasmin Convertible

Identification: Open-topped derivative of Tasmin two-seater coupe incorporating removable central roof section and collapsible rear section.

Engine: Front-mounted, V-6-cylinder with pushrod-operated overhead valves and Bosch K-Jetronic fuel injection. Bore × stroke 93 × 68.5 mm, displacement 2792 cc. Output 120 kW (160 bhp) @ 5700 rpm, torque 224 Nm (162 lb ft) @ 4300 rpm.

Transmission: Single-dry-plate clutch and four-speed manual gearbox, three-speed automatic transmission optional extra. Rear-wheel drive.

Suspension: Front, independent with wishbones, coil springs, telescopic shock absorbers and anti-roll bar. Rear, independent with trailing arms, fixed-length drive shafts, coil springs and telescopic shock absorbers.

Steering: Rack and pinion.

Brakes: Discs front and rear, servo-assisted.

Tyres: 205/60 VR–14.

Dimensions: Length 4013 mm (158 in), width 1728 mm (68 in), height 1192 mm (47 in), wheelbase 2387 mm (94 in).

Unladen weight: Approx. 1075 kg (2369 lb).

Notes: Standard equipment includes stereo radio/cassette player, electric aerial, electric window lifts and velour-trimmed upholstery.

VAUXHALL (GB)　　　Astra GL Hatchback

Identification: First saloon version of front-wheel-drive Vauxhall based on Opel Kadett and powered by 1.3-litre engine, since supplemented by L version.

Engine: Front and transverse-mounted four-cylinder in-line with belt-driven overhead camshaft and GM carburettor. Bore × stroke 75 × 73.4 mm, displacement 1297 cc. Output 55 kW (75 bhp) @ 5800 rpm, torque 103 Nm (74 lb ft) @ 3800 rpm.

Transmission: Single-dry-plate clutch and four-speed manual gearbox. Front-wheel drive.

Suspension: Front, independent with MacPherson struts, coil springs, telescopic shock absorbers and anti-roll bar. Rear, dead axle with trailing arms, coil springs, telescopic shock absorbers and anti-roll bar.

Steering: Rack and pinion.

Brakes: Discs front, drums rear, servo-assisted.

Tyres: 155 SR–13.

Dimensions: Length 4000 mm (157.5 in), width 1638 mm (64.5 in), height 1384 mm (54.5 in), wheelbase 2515 mm (99 in).

Unladen weight: 855 kg (1884 lb).

Notes: Standard equipment includes velour upholstery, radio, remote-control exterior mirror and hinged rear parcels shelf.

VAUXHALL (GB)   Astra L Estate

Identification: Estate derivative of Astra five-door L Hatchback with 1.3-litre engine and front-wheel drive.

Engine: Front and transverse-mounted four-cylinder in-line with belt-driven overhead camshaft and GM carburettor. Bore × stroke 75 × 73.4 mm, displacement 1297 cc. Output 55 kW (75 bhp) @ 5800 rpm, torque 103 Nm (74 lb ft) @ 3800 rpm.

Transmission: Single-dry-plate clutch and four-speed manual gearbox. Front-wheel drive.

Suspension: Front, independent with MacPherson struts, coil springs, telescopic shock absorbers and anti-roll bar. Rear, dead axle with trailing arms, coil springs, telescopic shock absorbers and anti-roll bar.

Steering: Rack and pinion.

Brakes: Discs front, drums rear, servo-assisted.

Tyres: 155 SR–13.

Dimensions: Length 4210 mm (165.7 in), width 1638 mm (64.5 in), height 1400 mm (55.1 in), wheelbase 2515 mm (99 in).

Unladen weight: 905 kg (1995 lb).

Notes: Standard equipment includes reclining front seats with head restraints, carpets, rear screen wash/wipe and electric engine fan.

VAUXHALL (GB)

Cavalier 2000 GLS
Sports Hatch

Identification: Top model in range of three-door hatchbacks based on Cavalier two-door and four-door saloons and supplementing 1600 GL and GLS models.

Engine: Front-mounted four-cylinder in-line with chain-driven overhead camshaft and GM carburettor. Bore × stroke 95 × 69.8 mm, displacement 1979 cc. Output 75 kW (100 bhp) @ 5400 rpm, torque 156 Nm (113 lb ft) @ 3800 rpm.

Transmission: Single-dry-plate clutch and four-speed manual gearbox, three-speed automatic transmission optional extra. Rear-wheel drive.

Suspension: Front, independent with wishbones, coil springs, telescopic shock absorbers and anti-roll bar. Rear, live axle with trailing arms, torque tube, coil springs, telescopic shock absorbers and anti-roll bar.

Steering: Rack and pinion.

Brakes: Discs front, drums rear, servo-assisted.

Tyres: 185/70 HR–13.

Dimensions: Length 4336 mm (170.7 in), width 1654 mm (65.1 in), height 1278 mm (50.3 in), wheelbase 2517 mm (99.1 in).

Unladen weight: 1030 kg (2270 lb).

Notes: Standard equipment includes velour seats and trim, carpeted load area, folding rear seat, halogen headlamps and radio.

VAUXHALL (GB)

Carlton 2000

Identification: Saloon version of model bridging gap between Cavalier and Viceroy and based on Opel Rekord, also available as five-door estate car.

Engine: Front-mounted four-cylinder in-line with chain-driven overhead camshaft and GM carburettor. Bore × stroke 95 × 69.8 mm, displacement 1979 cc. Output 75 kW (100 bhp) @ 5400 rpm, torque 160 Nm (116 lb ft) @ 3600 rpm.

Transmission: Single-dry-plate clutch and four-speed manual gearbox, three-speed automatic transmission optional extra. Rear-wheel drive.

Suspension: Front, independent with MacPherson struts, coil springs, telescopic shock absorbers and anti-roll bar. Rear, live axle with trailing arms, Panhard rod, coil springs, telescopic shock absorbers and anti-roll bar.

Steering: Recirculating ball, power-assistance optional extra.

Brakes: Discs front, drums rear, servo-assisted.

Tyres: 175 SR–14.

Dimensions: Length 4742 mm (186.7 in), width 1726 mm (68 in), height 1361 mm (53.6 in), wheelbase 2667 mm (105 in).

Unladen weight: 1130 kg (2491 lb).

Notes: Standard equipment includes velour-faced upholstery, head restraints, radio and height-adjustable driver's seat.

VAUXHALL (D) Viceroy

Identification: New intermediate executive saloon bridging gap between Carlton and Royale four-door models and based on modified Carlton bodyshell with six-cylinder engine.

Engine: Front-mounted six-cylinder in-line with chain-driven overhead camshaft and Zenith carburettor. Bore × stroke 87 × 69.8 mm, displacement 2490 cc. Output 85 kW (115 bhp) @ 5200 rpm, torque 179 Nm (132 lb ft) @ 3800 rpm.

Transmission: Single-dry-plate clutch and four-speed manual gearbox, four-speed-and-overdrive gearbox or three-speed automatic transmission optional extra. Rear-wheel drive.

Suspension: Front, independent with MacPherson struts, coil springs, telescopic shock absorbers and anti-roll bar. Rear, live axle with four-link system, coil springs, telescopic shock absorbers and anti-roll bar.

Steering: Recirculating ball, power-assisted.

Brakes: Discs front, drums rear, servo-assisted

Tyres: 195/70 HR–14.

Dimensions: Length 4732 mm (186.3 in), width 1722 mm (67.8 in), height 1410 mm (55.5 in), wheelbase 2667 mm (105 in).

Unladen weight: 1220 kg (2690 lb).

Notes: Standard equipment includes radio/cassette player, velour upholstery, height-adjustable driver's seat, central door locking and front seat head restraints.

VOLKSWAGEN (D)　　　　　　Polo GLS

Identification: Top model in three-car range of three-door hatchback saloons, supplementing 895 cc-engined N and L models offered with simpler specification, and incorporating detail improvements.

Engine: Front and transverse-mounted four-cylinder in-line with belt-driven overhead camshaft and Solex carburettor. Bore × stroke 69.5 × 72 mm, displacement 1093 cc. Output 37 kW (50 bhp) @ 5900 rpm, torque 75 Nm (56 lb ft) @ 3500 rpm.

Transmission: Single-dry-plate clutch and four-speed manual gearbox. Front-wheel drive.

Suspension: Front, independent with MacPherson struts, coil springs, telescopic shock absorbers and anti-roll bar. Rear, independent with trailing arms, coil springs and telescopic shock absorbers.

Steering: Rack and pinion.

Brakes: Discs front, drums rear, servo-assisted.

Tyres: 145 SR–13.

Dimensions: Length 3510 mm (138.2 in), width 1560 mm (61.4 in), height 1344 mm (52.9 in), wheelbase 2329 mm (91.7 in).

Unladen weight: 685 kg (1510 lb).

Notes: Standard equipment includes laminated screen, front and rear seats belts, fabric upholstery and head restraints.

VOLKSWAGEN (D)

Golf GLS

Identification: Reintroduced model to bridge gap between 1.3-litre and 1.6-litre Golf saloons and supplementing L version.

Engine: Front and transverse-mounted four-cylinder in-line with belt-driven overhead camshaft and Solex carburettor. Bore × stroke 79.5 × 73.4 mm, displacement 1457 cc. Output 52 kW (70 bhp) @ 5600 rpm, torque 104 Nm (75 lb ft) @ 3500 rpm.

Transmission: Single-dry-plate clutch and four-speed manual gearbox, three-speed automatic transmission optional extra. Front-wheel drive.

Suspension: Front, independent with MacPherson struts, coil springs, telescopic shock absorbers and anti-roll bar. Rear, independent with trailing arms, torsion beam, coil springs and telescopic shock absorbers.

Steering: Rack and pinion.

Brakes: Discs front, drums rear, servo-assisted.

Tyres: 155 SR–13.

Dimensions: Length 3720 mm (146.5 in), width 1613 mm (63.5 in), height 1410 mm (55.5 in), wheelbase 2400 mm (94.5 in).

Unladen weight: 775 kg (1708 lb).

Notes: Standard equipment includes folding rear seat, rear screen wash/wipe, remote-controlled rear-view mirror and locking fuel-filler cap.

VOLKSWAGEN (D)   Golf Convertible GLi

Identification: Karmann-bodied open-topped version of Golf powered by fuel-injected 1.6-litre engine also used in GTi saloon.

Engine: Front and transverse-mounted four-cylinder in-line with belt-driven overhead camshaft and Bosch K-Jetronic fuel injection. Bore × stroke 79.5 × 80 mm, displacement 1588 cc. Output 81 kW (110 bhp) @ 6100 rpm, torque 140 Nm (103 lb ft) @ 5000 rpm.

Transmission: Single-dry-plate clutch and five-speed manual gearbox. Front-wheel drive.

Suspension: Front, independent with MacPherson struts, coil springs, telescopic shock absorbers and anti-roll bar. Rear, independent with trailing arms, torsion bars, coil springs and telescopic shock absorbers.

Steering: Rack and pinion.

Brakes: Ventilated discs front, drums rear, servo-assisted.

Tyres: 175/70 HR–13.

Dimensions: Length 3815 mm (150.2 in), width 1628 mm (64.1 in), height 1394 mm (54.9 in), wheelbase 2400 mm (94.5 in).

Unladen weight: 940 kg (2072 lb).

Notes: Standard equipment includes heated glass rear screen, padded roll-over bar, alloy wheels, halogen headlamps and weather-resistant velour upholstery.

VOLKSWAGEN (D)

Jetta 1.5 GLS

Identification: Intermediate-size version of Jetta range of four-door saloons derived from Golf hatchbacks and bridging gap between 1.3-litre L and GL and 1.6-litre GLi. 1.5 LS model also available with lower level of equipment.

Engine: Front and transverse-mounted four-cylinder in-line with belt-driven overhead camshaft and Solex carburettor. Bore × stroke 79.5 × 73.4 mm, displacement 1457 cc. Output 52 kW (70 bhp) @ 5600 rpm, torque 113 Nm (81 lb ft) @ 3500 rpm.

Transmission: Single-dry-plate clutch and four-speed manual gearbox, three-speed automatic transmission optional extra. Front-wheel drive.

Suspension: Front, independent with MacPherson struts, coil springs, telescopic shock absorbers and anti-roll bar. Rear, semi-independent with torsion beam, trailing arms, coil springs, telescopic shock absorbers and anti-roll bar.

Steering: Rack and pinion.

Brakes: Discs front, drums rear, servo-assisted.

Tyres: 175/70 SR–13.

Dimensions: Length 4190 mm (165 in), width 1608 mm (63.3 in), height 1410mm (55.5 in), wheelbase 2398 mm (94.4 in).

Unladen weight: 825 kg (1818 lb).

Notes: Standard equipment includes cloth upholstery, front head restraints, centre console and wheelarch covers.

VOLKSWAGEN (D)   Scirocco GLS

Identification: Standard model in three-car range of two-plus-two coupes, supplementing fuel-injected GTi and Storm versions and featuring Giugiaro-styled bodywork.

Engine: Front and transverse-mounted four-cylinder in-line with belt-driven overhead camshaft and Solex carburettor. Bore × stroke 79.5 × 80 mm, displacement 1588 cc. Output 64 kW (85 bhp) @ 5600 rpm, torque 120 Nm (87 lb ft) @ 3200 rpm.

Transmission: Single-dry-plate clutch and four-speed manual gearbox, three-speed automatic transmission optional extra. Front-wheel drive.

Suspension: Front, independent with MacPherson struts, coil springs, telescopic shock absorbers and anti-roll bar. Rear, independent with trailing arms, torsion bars, coil springs, telescopic shock absorbers and anti-roll bar.

Steering: Rack and pinion.

Brakes: Discs front, drums rear, servo-assisted.

Tyres: 175/70 SR–13.

Dimensions: Length 3890 mm (153.2 in), width 1623 mm (63.9 in), height 1310 mm (51.6 in), wheelbase 2400 mm (94.5 in).

Unladen weight: 800 kg (1764 lb).

Notes: Standard equipment includes fabric upholstery, head restraints, rear screen wash/wipe, integral front and rear spoilers and alloy wheels.

VOLKSWAGEN (D)   Passat LD Estate

Identification: Diesel-engined derivative of petrol-engined Passat range with similar level of interior equipment and trim as LS model.

Engine: Front-mounted four-cylinder in-line with belt-driven overhead camshaft and Bosch diesel injection. Bore × stroke 76.5 × 80 mm, displacement 1471 cc. Output 37 kW (50 bhp) @ 5000 rpm, torque 80 Nm (59 lb ft) @ 3000 rpm.

Transmission: Single dry-plate clutch and four-speed manual gearbox. Front-wheel drive.

Suspension: Front, independent with MacPherson struts, coil springs, telescopic shock absorbers and anti-roll bar. Rear, dead axle with trailing arms, coil springs, telescopic shock absorbers and anti-roll bar.

Steering: Rack and pinion.

Brakes: Discs front, drums rear, servo-assisted.

Tyres: 155 SR–13.

Dimensions: Length 4265 mm (167.9 in), width 1610 mm (63.4 in), height 1360 mm (53.5 in), wheelbase 2470 mm (97.2 in).

Unladen weight: 945 kg (2083 lb).

Notes: Standard equipment includes reclining seats, head restraints, folding rear seat and heated rear screen.

Identification: Additional limited-edition top-of-the-range Passat estate car based on 1.6-litre GLS model with additional equipment.

Engine: Front-mounted four-cylinder in-line with belt-driven overhead camshaft and Solex carburettor. Bore × stroke 79.5 × 80 mm, displacement 1588 cc. Output 64 kW (85 bhp) @ 5600 rpm, torque 120 Nm (87 lb ft) @ 3200 rpm.

Transmission: Single-dry-plate clutch and four-speed manual gearbox, three-speed automatic transmission optional extra. Front-wheel drive.

Suspension: Front, independent with MacPherson struts, coil springs, telescopic shock absorbers and anti-roll bar. Rear, dead axle with trailing arms, coil springs, telescopic shock absorbers and anti-roll bar.

Steering: Rack and pinion.

Brakes: Discs front, drums rear, servo-assisted.

Tyres: 175/70 SR–13.

Dimensions: Length 4265 mm (167.9 in), width 1610 mm (63.4 in), height 1360 mm (53.5 in), wheelbase 2470 mm (97.2 in).

Unladen weight: 920 kg (2028 lb).

Notes: Standard equipment includes steel sun roof, alloy wheels, chromed wheelarches, radio/cassette player and velour upholstery.

Identification: Five-door derivative of three-door 343 saloon offered with choice of manual or automatic transmission and fixed or sun roof and incorporating minor styling changes.

Engine: Front-mounted four-cylinder in-line with pushrod-operated overhead valves and Weber carburettor. Bore × stroke 76 × 77 mm, displacement 1397 cc. Output 52 kW (70 bhp) @ 5500 rpm, torque 109 Nm (79 lb ft) @ 3500 rpm.

Transmission: Single-dry-plate clutch and four-speed manual gearbox, belt-driven automatic transmission optional extra. Rear-wheel drive.

Suspension: Front, independent with MacPherson struts, coil springs, telescopic shock absorbers and anti-roll bar. Rear, de Dion axle with trailing arms, semi-elliptic springs and telescopic shock absorbers.

Steering: Rack and pinion.

Brakes: Discs front, drums rear, servo-assisted.

Tyres: 155 SR–13.

Dimensions: Length 4205 mm (165.6 in), width 1660 mm (65.4 in), height 1392 mm (54.8 in), wheelbase 2395 mm (94.3 in).

Unladen weight: 1035 kg (2281 lb).

Notes: Engine convertible at extra cost to run on LPG through Landi-Hartog equipment and normal carburettor with dashboard-mounted dual-fuel changeover switch.

VOLVO (S)

244 DL

Identification: Lowest-priced model in revised 240-series range of saloons incorporating new front-end styling and interior modifications including new dashboard and control layout.

Engine: Front-mounted four-cylinder in-line with belt-driven overhead camshaft and Zenith carburettor. Bore × stroke 92 × 80 mm, displacement 2127 cc. Output 79 kW (107 bhp) @ 5500 rpm, torque 170 Nm (125 lb ft) @ 2500 rpm.

Transmission: Single-dry-plate clutch and four-speed manual gearbox, three-speed automatic transmission optional extra. Rear-wheel drive.

Suspension: Front, independent with MacPherson struts, coil springs, telescopic shock absorbers and anti-roll bar. Rear, live axle with trailing arms, coil springs, telescopic shock absorber and anti-roll bar.

Steering: Rack and pinion.

Brakes: Discs front and rear, servo-assisted.

Tyres: 165 SR–14.

Dimensions: Length 4790 mm (188.4 in), width 1710 mm (67.7 in), height 1430 mm (56.5 in), wheelbase 2640 mm (104 in).

Unladen weight: 1270 kg (2800 lb).

Notes: Standard equipment includes reclining seats, head restraints, laminated screen, headlamp wash/wipe and heated driver's seat.

Identification: Top model in revised 240-series range of estate cars incorporating front and rear styling changes and interior modifications.

Engine: Front-mounted four-cylinder in-line with belt-driven overhead camshaft and Bosch K-Jetronic fuel injection. Bore × stroke 92 × 80 mm, displacement 2127 cc. Output 92 kW (123 bhp) @ 5500 rpm, torque 170 Nm (125 lb ft) @ 3500 rpm.

Transmission: Single-dry-plate clutch and four-speed manual gearbox with overdrive, three-speed automatic transmission optional extra. Rear-wheel drive.

Suspension: Front, independent with MacPherson struts, coil springs, telescopic shock absorbers and anti-roll bar. Rear, live axle with trailing arms, coil springs, telescopic shock absorbers and anti-roll bar.

Steering: Rack and pinion, power-assisted to special order.

Brakes: Discs front and rear, servo-assisted.

Tyres: 185 HR–14.

Dimensions: Length 4790 mm (188.4 in), width 1710 mm (67.1 in), height 1460 mm (57.5 in), wheelbase 2640 mm (104 in).

Unladen weight: 1320 kg (2909 lb).

Notes: Standard equipment includes leather upholstery, rear screen wash/wipe, electric front window lifts and tinted glass.

VOLVO (S)   244 GLT

Identification: High-performance model of revised 240-series range of four-door saloons incorporating exterior styling changes and revised interior.

Engine: Front-mounted four-cylinder in-line with belt-driven overhead camshaft and Bosch K-Jetronic fuel injection. Bore × stroke 96 × 80 mm, displacement 2315 cc. Output 102 kW (136 bhp) @ 5500 rpm, torque 190 Nm (140 lb ft) @ 4500 rpm.

Transmission: Single-dry-plate clutch and four-speed manual gearbox with overdrive. Rear-wheel drive.

Suspension: Front, independent with MacPherson struts, coil springs, telescopic shock absorbers and anti-roll bar. Rear, live axle with trailing arms, coil springs, telescopic shock absorbers and anti-roll bar.

Steering: Rack and pinion, power-assisted.

Brakes: Discs front and rear, servo-assisted.

Tyres: 195/60 HR–15.

Dimensions: Length 4790 mm (188.4 in), width 1710 mm (67.1 in), height 1430 mm (56.5 in), wheelbase 2640 mm (104 in).

Unladen weight: 1310 kg (2887 lb).

Notes: Standard equipment includes sun roof, spoiler, alloy wheels, metallic paintwork and tinted glass.

Identification: Larger-engined replacement for 2.6-litre-engined 264 GLE incorporating styling changes and featuring very high level of interior equipment.

Engine: Front-mounted V-6-cylinder with belt-driven overhead camshaft and Bosch K-Jetronic fuel injection. Bore × stroke 91 × 73 mm, displacement 2849 cc. Output 114 kW (155 bhp) @ 5500 rpm, torque 230 Nm (170 lb ft) @ 3000 rpm.

Transmission: Single-dry-plate clutch and four-speed manual gearbox with overdrive, three-speed automatic transmission optional extra. Rear-wheel drive.

Suspension: Front, independent with MacPherson struts, coil springs, telescopic shock absorbers and anti-roll bar. Rear, live axle with trailing arms, coil springs, telescopic shock absorbers and anti-roll bar.

Steering: Rack and pinion, power-assisted.

Brakes: Discs front and rear, servo-assisted.

Tyres: 185/70 HR–14.

Dimensions: Length 4790 mm (188.4 in), width 1710 mm (67.1 in), height 1430 mm (56.5 in), wheelbase 2640 mm (104 in).

Unladen weight: 1495 kg (3295 lb).

Notes: Standard equipment includes air-conditioning, electric window lifts, electrically adjustable rear-view mirrors, rear head restraints and rear window sun blinds.

Identification: 260-series estate car with latest 2.8-litre fuel injected engine, supplementing higher-specification GLE version and incorporating front and rear styling changes.

Engine: Front-mounted V-6-cylinder with belt-driven overhead camshaft and Bosch K-Jetronic fuel injection. Bore × stroke 91 × 73 mm, displacement 2849 cc. Output 114 kW (155 bhp) @ 5500 rpm, torque 230 Nm (170 lb ft) @ 3000 rpm.

Transmission: Single-dry-plate clutch and four-speed manual gearbox with overdrive, three-speed automatic transmission optional extra. Rear-wheel drive.

Suspension: Front, independent with MacPherson struts, coil springs, telescopic shock absorbers and anti-roll bar. Rear, live axle with trailing arms, coil springs, telescopic shock absorbers and anti-roll bar.

Steering: Rack and pinion, power-assisted.

Brakes: Discs front and rear, servo-assisted.

Tyres: 185/70 HR–14.

Dimensions: Length 4790 mm (188.4 in), width 1710 mm (67.1 in), height 1460 mm (57.5 in), wheelbase 2640 mm (104 in).

Unladen weight: 1555 kg (3427 lb).

Notes: Standard equipment includes tinted glass, metallic paint, leather upholstery, rear screen wash/wipe, central locking and spoiler.